ACHIEVING QTS

CROSS-CURRICULAR STRAND

CHILDREN'S SPIRITUAL, MORAL, SOCIAL AND CULTURAL DEVELOPMENT

2

ACHIEVING QTS
CROSS-CURRICULAR STRAND

Children's Spiritual, Moral, Social and Cultural Development: Primary and Early Years

Tony Eaude

Learning Matters

First published in 2006 by Learning Matters Ltd.

British Library Cataloguing in Publication Data
A CIP record for this book is available from the British Library

ISBN-13: 978 1 84445 048 0
ISBN-10: 1 84445 048 1

Cover design by Topics – The Creative Partnership
Project management by Deer Park Productions, Tavistock
Typeset by PDQ Typesetting Ltd, Newcastle under Lyme
Printed and bound in Great Britain by Bell & Bain Ltd, Glasgow

Learning Matters Ltd
33 Southernhay East
Exeter EX1 1NX
Tel: 01392 215560
Email: info@learningmatters.co.uk
www.learningmatters.co.uk

CONTENTS

THE AUTHOR

Dr Tony Eaude was a teacher and head teacher for over 20 years, working initially in a special school and then in suburban, new town and multicultural primary schools. He completed a master's degree in Educational Research Methodology and a Doctorate at the University of Oxford on how teachers of four and five year old children understand spiritual development.

Other publications which he has written include three short books, one as a co-author, in a series for parent, several booklets for teachers, including 'New Perspectives on Spiritual Development' and 'Values Education – developing positive attitudes', and a range of academic and practical articles on related subjects.

Tony Eaude now works as an independent research consultant, evaluating educational programmes, leading training, supporting teacher research and policy development and writing both for teachers and for an academic audience. He teaches part-time in an urban primary school. More details of his work can be seen on www.edperspectives.org.uk

Tony welcomes feedback about the contents of this book and may be contacted by email at tony.eaude@green.ox.ac.uk.

This book is designed to introduce you to one of the most fascinating aspects of teaching young children – spiritual, moral, social and cultural development, usually shortened to SMSC. You may be unsure quite what this means, let alone how to teach it. By the end of this book, I hope that you will have gained new insights into what SMSC is all about and feel more confident about how to make provision for it.

I decided to teach in primary schools because I wanted to work with children at a formative stage of their lives and to teach the 'whole child', not just one subject. Even after 30 years – as a class teacher, subject co-ordinator, deputy head and (for nine years) a headteacher – this remains a source of both continuing challenge and great personal fulfilment. I have tried to draw on this experience, and my recent work as a researcher, to help you recognise and meet the challenges and share this fulfilment.

As a teacher, you can help to enrich and transform children's lives. Teaching them to be confident and competent readers, writers and mathematicians is part of this. However, SMSC deals with much more elusive aspects of personal development: how to make sense of the world and other people; how to interact with other people; the sort of person one is and may become (which runs through every subject area and every aspect of school life). Your values and beliefs are crucial in how well you make provision for SMSC. This may strike you as rather daunting, but as a teacher you are not just a deliverer of information. There is no point being an expert in the techniques of teaching but being dissatisfied that you are not getting to the heart of what matters most. Teachers help to shape the values, attitudes and character of the next generation.

You will reach a greater understanding of what SMSC means and how it links with the rest of children's learning if you:

- **recognise how SMSC fits into wider contexts of the law and the curriculum;**
- **think about and develop a new understanding of the distinctive features of 'spiritual', 'moral', 'social' and 'cultural' as facets of personal development;**
- **see the common themes and the wider implications for children's learning.**

Chapter 1 addresses the first point, Chapters 2 to 5 the second and Chapter 6 the third.

The second half of the book turns more to the practical implications of making good provision for SMSC, with Chapter 7 exploring learning environments, Chapter 8 teaching approaches and Chapter 9 showing how SMSC can be integrated across the whole curriculum and the implications for planning. In Chapter 10, I discuss the link between your own personal and professional development and how you can enhance children's SMSC.

Throughout the book I refer to the Standards to Achieve Qualified Teacher Status and to a range of Government documents and the National Curriculum. To help you consider how children learn, I provide illustrative stories, case studies and short summaries of relevant research to introduce key ideas and raise questions and points for consideration and discussion, to encourage you to link your own experience with a wider base of experience and thought. The style adopted is designed to encourage you to reflect on, and question, your own assumptions and beliefs. Most chapters end with some recommended reading, and a short commentary on each example, to help you decide if you want to consult these, as well as a more conventional list of references.

You will find this book rather different from others on your course. I offer examples and advice about what you might do differently, but I do not recommend lists of activities. I am sure that, at times, you will feel frustrated at this. One reason is that, while teaching involves setting up activities, SMSC depends much more on *how* you teach than *what* you teach. So, my aim is to help you to understand the underlying reasons why SMSC is so important, not simply to offer 'tips for teachers'. SMSC does not lend itself to an approach based on a series of lessons. A second reason is that your provision for SMSC will depend on your values and beliefs, and those of your school community. I cannot decide these for you but I hope to help you to explore them. A third reason is that your own provision will be affected by many other variables. For example, although I highlight the different needs of older and younger age-groups, where appropriate, I tend to consider the age range from when children start school until eleven years old as a whole. You will benefit most by relating what I have written to your own context, personal experience and practice as a teacher and a person.

This book is based on research and experience. Many teachers are wary of educational research, partly because they are busy people and research is often regarded as being inaccessible. A more profound reason is that research tends to add to complexity. Too much complexity *can* get in the way of knowing what to do next Tuesday morning or distract one's attention from simple, but important, truths. However, if teaching is seen as little more than applied common sense, we fail to draw on other people's collective wisdom and, as individuals or as a profession, may become vulnerable to the latest fad.

This book offers few easy answers. Of course, you will decide how you read the book, whether straight through, dipping in and out, or considering the questions and points for consideration and discussion on your own or with others or not at all! But let me make three suggestions:

- **do not believe that the questions posed have only one answer, as this can easily get in the way;**

- **read quite slowly and reflectively, dwelling on the questions and points raised, discussing these with other students, friends and colleagues; and**

- **as you read, reflect on the aims of education because a consideration of SMSC shows that there is much more to education than good results in National Tests.**

I hope that you will find this a challenging and an enjoyable read and that, by the end, you will have some answers and many more questions and ideas. These will help you become a more reflective practitioner during your training and implant good habits for your future development in one of the most fascinating aspects of teaching.

Tony Eaude
March 2006
tony.eaude@green.ox.ac.uk

1 WHY IS SPIRITUAL, MORAL, SOCIAL AND CULTURAL DEVELOPMENT IMPORTANT?

By the end of this chapter you should:

- realise the significance of the Standards for the Award of Qualified Teacher Status and the place of spiritual, moral, social and cultural development (SMSC) in them;
- know about the place of SMSC and other facets of personal development in recent Education Acts, the National Curriculum and the Ofsted Framework;
- have been introduced to how SMSC is linked to children's learning and attainment;
- realise that good provision for SMSC cannot be dissociated from your own values and what you believe the aims of education to be.

This will help you to meet Standards:
→ S 1.1, 1.2, 1.3, 1.5, 1.7, 1.8, 2.2, 2.4, 3.3.14

You will have all sorts of reasons for becoming a primary school teacher. Other people on your course will share some of these and also have their own. You are all starting on a challenging, fascinating and worthwhile journey. These reasons probably do not relate to becoming rich or powerful in the conventional sense. But you can enrich young children's lives and be influential in one of the most important tasks imaginable – how the next generation grows up and the sort of people they become.

How do you become a primary school teacher?

The formal requirements for you to achieve Qualified Teacher Status (QTS) are set out in DfES/TTA (2002). These Standards are set by the Department for Education and Skills and the Training and Development Agency for Schools (TDA), formerly the Teacher Training Agency (TTA). You have to meet all of the Standards relevant to your own subject and phase to be awarded QTS. I highlight which Standards each chapter will help you to meet. By the time you read this, the exact wording, and possibly the numbers, may have changed slightly, but the overall structure should remain much the same.

Your course will provide a range of experiences, depending on your own background, qualifications and skills, but these are likely to include:

- opportunities through lectures and discussion to develop your understanding of how young children learn;
- specific teaching to extend your subject knowledge and skills;
- advice on the practicalities of how to teach, such as planning appropriate activities, managing classroom behaviour and assessing what children have learnt;

- **teaching practice, under the supervision of an experienced teacher and with advice and support from your tutors.**

Inevitably, you bring to your teaching a theory – or set of underlying beliefs – about how children learn, which, in turn, affects how you teach. It is changing, or elaborating, or refining these beliefs that helps you to become a better teacher, especially in relation to SMSC. Many of these beliefs are unconscious. Polanyi (cited in Schon, 1987, p22) coined the term 'tacit knowledge' to describe what makes a good teacher (or plumber or scientist). Much of this – how to include a reticent child, or ask a question that draws on, and extends, a group's understanding – is hard to spot and even harder to learn. Making your tacit knowledge explicit can help you to think about, and so change, your beliefs and your approach to teaching. The first part of this book is intended to help you to uncover, and think about, the underlying beliefs that you, and others, hold, and to reflect on how these affect, and can be affected by, your experience in the classroom.

You may think that, once you have gained QTS and secured your first job, you have done all that you need to be a teacher. In one sense, this is true and expectations of you will be high – from colleagues, parents and children. But a good teacher never stops developing. This is recognised in the support that your school should offer – through courses, mentoring and chances to take on new responsibilities, for instance – when you are newly qualified. But, once this specific programme comes to an end, your development as a teacher is far from over. You wouldn't want your teeth filled by a dentist, or travel over a bridge built by an engineer, who didn't update his or her skills. Good teachers are always doing so by becoming, increasingly, 'reflective practitioners'.

Pollard and Tann (1994, pp9–10) identify six main features of reflective teaching:

- **an active concern with aims and consequences;**
- **a process in which teachers monitor, evaluate and revise their own practice continuously;**
- **competence in methods of classroom enquiry;**
- **attitudes of open-mindedness, responsibility and wholeheartedness;**
- **teacher judgment, informed both by self-reflection and insights from educational disciplines; and**
- **collaboration and dialogue with colleagues.**

Learning to be a teacher involves, initially, a concentration on the mechanics of teaching. However, good pedagogy involves more than simply becoming proficient in these. You will become a more reflective and a better teacher, if you can relate your teaching to the messages in your course, and in this book, so that practice, informed by theory and theoretical knowledge, is brought to life by the reality you face in the classroom.

How does spiritual, moral, social and cultural development fit into the standards for QTS?

The Standards for Achieving QTS are organised in three interrelated sections: professional values and practice (SI), knowledge and understanding (S2) and teaching (S3). SI relates especially to 'attitudes and commitment', highlighting how important it is to:

- respect social, cultural, linguistic, religious and ethnic backgrounds (SI.I);
- treat pupils consistently, with respect and consideration (SI.2); and
- demonstrate and promote the positive values, attitudes and behaviour (expected) from pupils (SI.3).

It is no accident that these are the first three sections in the Standards. The (much longer) competencies related to teaching are underpinned by those in the 'professional values and practice' and 'knowledge and understanding' Standards. These less measurable, more intangible aspects, and your own personal attitudes and commitment, are fundamental to becoming a good teacher.

However, the wording of the Standards makes little mention of SMSC. Neither 'spiritual' nor 'moral' appear at all. The words 'social' and 'cultural' do, six and four times respectively, but the only reference to these in terms of *development* comes in S2.4 where an understanding is required of 'how pupils' learning can be affected by their physical, intellectual, linguistic, social, cultural and emotional development.' This might be regarded as extraordinary, not least because, as we shall see, SMSC is very prominent both in the 1988 Education Act and the Office for Standards in Education (Ofsted) Framework for Inspection.

What does this tell us? All teachers care about how children develop both intellectually and personally. But how we teach involves decisions on priorities. The emphasis of the Standards seems to take for granted that:

- the aims of education are not contested, but mainly concerned with higher measurable outcomes in the core subjects;
- learning is mainly about acquiring information and skills, rather than developing attitudes, values and beliefs; and
- teaching should focus mainly on transmitting knowledge and skills, rather than drawing on children's capacity for learning and enriching their wider personal development.

These can be regarded as a simple example of what is meant by uncovering the underlying beliefs, the tacit assumptions implied in a particular action, or a document.

The specific competencies highlighted in the Standards and reflected in your course structure will, rightly, be your most immediate concern. But the aims of education have been, and always will be, matters for debate and there is a danger of concentrating too much on what can be measured. The evidence (which we shall consider) about how children learn best reveals how little we really know about this. Teaching is a complex process, involving much more than the delivery of information or what can be achieved by meeting only short-term objectives.

Points for consideration and discussion

What made you decide to become a teacher?

Which of your values and beliefs do you most wish your pupils to share?

To what extent is it right to pass on your values and beliefs to young children?

Why is SMSC important in your development as a teacher?

Apart from the Standards, there are at least three other main reasons why you should take SMSC seriously:

- **personal development (of which SMSC is a vital part) matters at least much as academic attainment in the development of 'the whole child';**
- **what, and how, children learn is more significant than what they are taught (though, hopefully, these are linked); and**
- **this will, probably, make you more fulfilled in relation to why you became a teacher and a better motivated teacher.**

I am reluctant to draw too sharp a distinction between academic learning and personal development, because children's emotional well-being and how well they learn are closely linked. For instance, children who are frightened of singing or of mathematics are unlikely to do well until they overcome this fear. Skills such as gymnastics or creating a website require confidence as well as technique. Working in a team involves self-awareness, empathy with other people, knowing when to step forward and when to hold back and other similar, intangible qualities. Theoretical training can enhance these, but greater proficiency is achieved mainly in doing the activity – just as in teaching.

It is tempting to think of what happens in the classroom as being mainly about what you, as a teacher, do. Your course will, rightly, emphasise the content of what you teach and the techniques of classroom management. If lessons are not well-planned, or behaviour is out of control, children's learning will be impeded. But, ultimately, education is about enabling children to learn. The National Curriculum tends to stress the content of what should be taught, with a strong emphasis on the core subjects of English, mathematics and science, and information and communications technology (ICT). This must be balanced with learning about the really important lessons for life – whom we can trust, how best to relate to each other, or whether those who love us continue to do so when we let them down. These aspects of SMSC are all crucial to personal development, mostly learnt implicitly rather than by direct instruction.

Most teachers in primary schools find enabling children's personal development to be one of the most enjoyable and fulfilling aspects of teaching. Part of your motivation in deciding to become a teacher may have been to improve the lives of young children and to extend the range of experiences and opportunities open to them. This is a wonderful aspect of the job. However, reality will soon kick in (if it hasn't already). Teaching is very demanding. Most classes are challenging in a variety of ways. Children offer a great deal, but also draw heavily on the teacher's emotional resources. Teachers work long hours, often at a cost to their own health. As you become more experienced, this will become (a bit) easier, but many teachers give up after a few years, often with their idealism squashed under a mountain of planning, assessment and recording. Recognising that there is more to teaching and to learning than what can be measured, and that young children need spiritual, moral, social and cultural, as well as intellectual, development, will help you become a better, and a more fulfilled, teacher.

What does the law say?

The 1944 Education Act stated that *it shall be the duty of the local education authority for every area, so far as their powers extend, to contribute towards the spiritual, moral, mental and physical development of the community* ... The 1988 Education Act, introducing the National Curriculum, required schools to provide for children's *spiritual, moral, cultural, mental and physical* development. The 1992 Education (Schools) Act, which led to the creation of Ofsted and the Framework for Inspection, revised this list to *spiritual, moral, social and cultural development,* separating, to some extent, personal from intellectual development. The Children Act (2004), based on the Green Paper 'Every Child Matters', includes mental and physical again, but omits the social aspect.

Elements of personal development are prominent in all this legislation, reflecting a long tradition that education is about far more than academic attainment. The change of wording resulted from fierce debate, reflecting changing beliefs about the role of education and about society. For instance, note the 1944 Act emphasis on the development of the community, and the 1988 Act on the school's role in children's development. The inclusion of 'cultural' in the 1988 and 1992 Acts probably reflects the growth of a more diverse society. We explore what these words mean in the next four chapters, but it is important to remember that the legislation emphasises these aspects of personal development and that the wording changes, slightly, even within a few years.

Points for consideration and discussion

What do you think that the principal aims of those educating young children should be? (Highlight three or four.)

What possible dangers follow from too great an emphasis on literacy and numeracy?

What dangers are associated with too great an emphasis on personal development?

What about the National Curriculum and Ofsted?

These laws provide the foundation for other, more detailed, guidance. The two most obvious are National Curriculum documentation and the Ofsted Framework for Inspection, both of which were revised as difficulties became apparent and priorities changed. The National Curriculum introduced 'core' and 'foundation' subjects. The core subjects were English, mathematics and science, the foundation subjects history, geography, art, music, physical education and technology, with Religious Education a compulsory subject but not part of the National Curriculum. The basic structure for Key Stages 1 and 2 has remained little changed, though Information and Communications Technology (ICT) is now more prominent. One problem was how underlying themes or strands fitted in – such as personal, social and health education (PSHE), citizenship or environmental awareness, which are subjects that cross subject boundaries, and others, such as equal opportunities or SMSC, which underlie every subject. The government's advisory bodies, the National Curriculum Council (NCC), the School Curriculum Assessment Authority (SCAA) and the Qualifications and Curriculum Authority (QCA) issued guidance on these strands and themes. Those relating to SMSC such as NCC (1993), Ofsted (1994), SCAA (1995, 1996) and QCA (1997) remain useful.

However, the difficulty runs deeper. SMSC challenges, in some respects, a curriculum conceived in separate subjects. The National Curriculum and its supporting documents, in emphasising content, mostly offers guidance on *what* to teach rather than *how* it is to be taught. However, as we shall see, process tends to matter more in themes and strands such as SMSC. Lessons will rarely focus only on SMSC, but every lesson brings opportunities for SMSC. Teachers need simultaneously to be aware of, and not to be constrained by, subject boundaries. Learning, especially in young children, is often less linear and more unpredictable than teachers think.

The Foundation Stage Curriculum, introduced in 2000, identifies six areas of learning:

- **personal, social and emotional development;**
- **communication, language and literacy;**
- **mathematical development;**
- **knowledge and understanding of the world;**
- **physical development; and**
- **creative development.**

This makes it easier to adopt an approach conducive to SMSC than a timetable based on definite boundaries between subjects.

Ofsted's Framework for Inspection, introduced after the 1992 Act, proved controversial in relation to SMSC for three main reasons. Firstly, there was no clear agreement on what terms like 'spiritual' and 'cultural' meant. Since what is inspected usually determines what schools and teachers focus on most, everyone wanted to know what inspectors were looking for. Secondly, inspection concentrated heavily on what could be measured, especially in literacy and numeracy. There is considerable doubt – to put it politely – whether provision for SMSC, let alone outcomes, can be judged like this. The key action points which schools have to address after an inspection rarely include any related to SMSC. Thirdly, the focus on literacy and numeracy led many schools to limit the range of curricular experiences and the time available for the foundation and more 'creative' subjects. The most recent change to the Framework, from September 2005, gives a greater emphasis than previously to personal development – children being safe and happy, and enjoying learning – reflecting the priorities of 'Every Child Matters'.

This explains, in terms of the law and government guidance, why teachers have to promote children's spiritual, moral, social and cultural development. But the real reason is more basic. Personal development matters at least as much as academic attainment. In Talbot and Tate's words (in Smith and Standish, 1997, pp1–2), *Which of us, after all, wants their child to leave school clutching a handful of certificates, but with no idea of how to be a human being?*

We shall return frequently to the aims and purposes of education. What teachers aim to achieve should always be a matter of debate, though too often it is not. The reflective teacher frequently considers these aims and how his or her teaching relates to them, both from day to day and over the long haul. I am tempted to try and answer this for you and, inevitably, the questions posed and examples given reflect my own view and seek to encourage you towards particular responses. However, teachers must find their own answers – none of which is ever final – to this question. This does not mean that you can just choose for yourself what to do as a teacher, since you must take account of the aims explicitly set out in the National Curriculum and in school policies. But, as we shall see, your own beliefs, values and attitudes will, deliberately or not, influence how you teach. You should not – and cannot – leave them behind as you enter the classroom. They will not only enrich children's learning, but can help you to achieve your ideals as a teacher. You will, without conscious effort, enhance children's SMSC by being who you are and the values that you impart.

Points for consideration and discussion

Which qualities would you look for in someone who is 'well educated'?

Who most influenced your own values and beliefs, and how?

What experiences do you bring to the classroom that might enhance children's SMSC? You do!

Isn't SMSC the same as personal development? How do they overlap and relate to each other?

We have seen how the prominence of elements of personal development changed in successive Education Acts. No one would seriously suggest that children's mental or physical development should be ignored since these were removed from one list, or emotional or aesthetic development because these were never included. Rather, priorities result from a refinement of broader categories, depending on which aspects of personal development and qualities are deemed especially important as social contexts change.

You may agree that personal development matters and see education as not just about academic attainment. But why use words like spiritual, moral, social and cultural? Do such puzzling and elusive ideas get in the way? Isn't it just a matter of developing the whole child? Lambourn (1996, p156) suggests that spiritual development is nothing more than *personal development in its fullest sense*. In one sense, this is true, but it doesn't get us anywhere because we still don't know what this involves.

Three of the four words (with social perhaps the exception) describe elusive, hard-to-grasp concepts. 'Spiritual' was deliberately left vague in the 1944 Act, when it would have been widely seen as synonymous with 'religious'. This became increasingly problematic with social and cultural changes from the 1960s onwards, but only after the introduction of inspection was the distinction between the two widely discussed. 'Moral' carries connotations (which I shall suggest are too limited) of teaching children the difference between right and wrong, in a context where politicians and parents worry about declining standards of behaviour. 'Cultural' is, as Eagleton (2000) suggests, one of the most slippery words in English, with several different meanings of 'culture' used interchangeably, often confusingly. They are 'essentially contested' concepts, whose meaning is widely disputed, with considerable difficulties in reaching adequate definitions.

It may be helpful to start by thinking of these four domains, or broad elements:

Spiritual		Meaning
Moral		Action
Social	relates to	Interaction
Cultural		Belonging

The next five chapters explore both what is distinctive about the four elements of SMSC and how they overlap. For example, social development depends on greater cultural awareness, spiritual development is closely linked with how one acts, i.e. moral development, which in turn depends on, and affects, social development and cannot be separated from cultural expectations as the following story illustrates:

Case study

Billy's story

As a headteacher, I spent a lot of time with a few children, often boys, who had got into trouble. Billy was one, a nine year old, who often hurt other children, sometimes when he lost his temper, at other times more deliberately. His background was very difficult, with his father and mother separated, an uncle in prison for drug-related offences, uncertainty about his ethnicity, and an upbringing marked by poverty and insecurity. Since his relationships with other children were poor, Billy's difficulty could be seen as social. His behaviour was aggressive and he showed little evidence of remorse, so maybe as moral. He did not know where he belonged, so maybe cultural. To me, he seemed more like someone who lacked meaning in his life, an absence that I called spiritual without quite knowing what I meant by that. But one could not make sense of Billy's relationships, behaviour, identity or lack of meaning without some understanding of how all were interlinked.

Does a greater emphasis on SMSC contribute to, or distract from, higher standards of attainment?

As we have seen, the Standards for Achieving QTS do not mention SMSC very prominently and schools are judged primarily by their results in literacy and numeracy. So, a key question is how SMSC is linked to raising standards, or whether it is at best peripheral, or at worst a distraction from the real business of education. This cannot be answered with any certainty, because there are so many variables to take into account. No robust quantitative link can be made between high scores and good provision for SMSC. Those whose main concern is to improve results in literacy and numeracy may see SMSC as a distraction from what really matters. Those who emphasise that education has broader and less measurable aims, as I do, worry that the 'standards agenda' leaves too little space for personal development.

The following chart points to some of the main differences:

The 'standards agenda' tends to emphasise:	SMSC tends to emphasise:
Content – what is learnt	Process – how what is learnt is learnt
The acquisition of skills and knowledge	Relationships, values and attitudes
Literacy and numeracy	Breadth of curriculum
Pace and challenge	Space for reflection
Measurable results	Outcomes which are hard to assess

This seems like a sharp divide. In some ways it is, but it is more helpful to see these as two sides of the same coin. As a teacher, you will need to take account of both and provide a broad and balanced curriculum. Few people would deny the importance of content, of skills or of pace, in providing challenge and maintaining motivation. Reflection helps both to deepen learning and to think about how information and experiences fit into the 'bigger picture'. Someone with a narrow range of interests is usually not regarded as well educated. And unless we can apply what we have learnt, our learning remains fenced off from the rest of our lives. But children's academic success is heavily influenced by how well their personal and emotional needs are met. Think how Billy's difficulties are bound to hamper his academic progress – worries about relationships or money hinder any of us from learning effectively.

Good provision for children's SMSC is concerned with relationships and values, slower and deeper learning, and longer-term results which can rarely be measured. While this cannot be shown conclusively to contribute directly to higher standards of attainment, it has the potential to do so through providing calmer learning environments where children:

- **are more confident about their own identity as active and creative learners;**
- **make connections between different domains of learning;**
- **become more reflective; and**
- **develop intrinsic motivation for their behaviour.**

However, whether good provision for SMSC leads to higher standards is really the wrong question, because the National Curriculum and the 'standards agenda' tend to assume that the aims of education are pre-determined and uncontested: that the main purpose of primary education is for children to learn to read and write fluently, and to manipulate numbers confidently. Put crudely, success is often measured by whether a child has reached at least Level 4 in English and mathematics by the age of 11. SMSC emphasises a much more complicated and interesting role for the teacher – helping children to understand themselves, to relate appropriately to other people and cultures, and to know how to act.

How can we learn more about SMSC?

Many aspects of learning, as we shall see, involve something more like a conversation than a lecture, a construction than a delivery. Because much of SMSC relates to elusive, often contested, issues, my aim is to elaborate, enrich and widen your understanding, rather than for you to accept everything that I write. I am aiming to:

- **persuade you that each element of SMSC describes a distinctive aspect of personal development;**

- **help you to see how these are linked both with each other and with the rest of children's learning; and**

- **suggest practical ways in which you can recognise opportunities for enhancing SMSC and integrate these in your teaching.**

Bruner (1996) describes learning as like a spiral, moving from simple to more complex understanding. When one's current understanding is challenged by new experience (or feedback), this leads to a changed, hopefully improved, understanding. So, knowledge is constructed on the foundations of what is already known, with this process described as elaboration. This does not mean more complicated; indeed, mathematicians and scientists often look for more elegant, or economical, explanations. Rather, elaboration emphasises working from the current state of the learner's knowledge. What one already knows greatly affects both how information is perceived, and how it is processed. Much important learning, as we shall see, 'bypasses' language. However, a more precise vocabulary helps us to think about what we are learning which, as Vygotsky (1978) discusses, enables 'higher-order' learning. Articulating one's understanding – and then doing so again and again, in the light of new experiences and ideas – helps both children and adults to learn. I hope to help you start from, and enrich, your present understanding, leading to an elaborated, but not convoluted, understanding.

You may have started your course – and this book – thinking of SMSC as rather a side-issue. I hope that, by now, you will agree that it relates to the most fundamental aspects of education. You may also have thought of it as a bit bland and uninteresting. Not so. The journey of exploration into what SMSC entails will, at times, challenge and unsettle you. This will help you realise that there is far more to teaching – and SMSC in particular – than may appear on the surface.

Recommended reading

DfES/TTA (2002) *Qualifying to Teach: Professional Standards for Qualified Teacher Status and Requirements for Initial Training*. For the updated Standards see www.tda.gov.uk

NCC (National Curriculum Council) (1993) *Spiritual and Moral Development: a discussion paper*. York: NCC

Ofsted (1994) *Spiritual, Moral, Social and Cultural Development*. London: Ofsted

QCA (Qualifications and Curriculum Authority) (1997) *The promotion of pupils' spiritual, moral, social and cultural development*. London: QCA

SCAA (School Curriculum and Assessment Authority) (1995) *Spiritual and Moral Development*. SCAA Discussion Papers No. 3 London, SCAA

SCAA (1996) *Education for adult life: the spiritual and moral development of young people: a summary report*. SCAA Discussion Papers No. 6 London: SCAA.
These five pamphlets are well worth looking at to see how the emphasis of guidance changes and to enrich your own understanding of SMSC.

Pollard, A and Tann, S (1994) *Reflective teaching in the Primary School*. London: Cassell. An interesting book about teaching as a whole, especially the section on reflective teaching (pp8–17).

Other references

Bruner, J (1996) *The Culture of Education*. Cambridge, MA: Harvard University Press

Children Act (2004) see www.everychildmatters.gov.uk/ete/primaryschool

Eagleton, T (2000) *The Idea of Culture*. Oxford: Blackwell

Lambourn, D (1996) 'Spiritual' minus 'personal-social' = ?: a critical note on an empty category, pp150–58, of R Best (ed) *Education, Spirituality and the Whole Child*. London: Cassell

Schon, D (1987) *Educating the Reflective Practitioner*. San Fransisco, CA: Jossey Bass

Smith, R and Standish, P (1997) *Teaching right and wrong – moral education in the balance*. Stoke on Trent: Trentham Books

Vygotsky, L (1978) *Mind in Society: the development of higher psychological processes*. Cambridge, MA: Harvard University Press

2 WHAT DOES SPIRITUAL DEVELOPMENT INVOLVE?

By the end of this chapter you should:

- know about alternative definitions of spiritual development, including Ofsted's;
- have broadened your idea of the type of questions with which spiritual development is concerned;
- understand the difference between spiritual experience and provision to enhance it;
- be considering where opportunities for spiritual development occur in different subjects and areas of school life.

This will help you to meet Standards:
- ◉ S 1.1, 1.2, 1.3, 1.7, 2.2, 2.4, 2.7, 3.3.1, 3.3.14

Can one define spiritual development?

'Spiritual' is probably the hardest of the four elements of SMSC to pin down and to define exactly. Carr (1995, p85) writes that *some precise definition of spiritual educa-tion ... is an extremely unpromising strategy to adopt.* It is not open to what philosophers call stipulative definition, with exact boundaries. The best comparison is with a concept such as 'games'. We all know what a game is, but try defining this precisely. This does not mean that it is not real or important. In this chapter, I try to enrich your current understanding by looking at common features of different approaches and discussing some possible misconceptions. There is a danger of using spiritual development to mean whatever one wants. Of course, one *can* do so, but a clearer, more widely shared, understanding of what we mean by spiritual develop-ment and experience helps to avoid some pitfalls when deciding on how to enhance it.

One good starting point is to explore what comes to mind when you think of spiritual development. So, please spend a few minutes thinking about what you think spiritual development is all about *for you* and note down your ideas.

If you are considering this in a group, compare notes. When I do this exercise with teachers, similar ideas recur time and again. These include:

- **religion and worship;**
- **relationships to each other and/or to God;**
- **evocative, or favourite, places and experiences;**
- **creativity and responses to art and music;**
- **mystery and what we can't really understand;**
- **prayer, silence and meditation;**
- **the opposite of what we can touch and feel (the material world);**

- experiences which take us beyond ourselves;
- what is everlasting, or transcendent, or ultimate.

You may wish to compare this with your list — not because they, or you, are 'right' — but because this provides an idea of the breadth of areas involved.

The following questions may also help to articulate your understanding:

- **Does the idea of a spiritually *mature* child, or adult, make sense to you? If so, what are the characteristics, or qualities, of such a person?**
- **Which sorts of activities inhibit spiritual development? (It is sometimes easier to think what something is *not*, rather than what it *is*.)**

Think of incidents from your own life as a child, or parent, or student, which you would describe as spiritual. 'Moments of significance' drawn from my experience of teaching include:

- **Oliver seeing a beautiful sunset that had helped him to recognise he was part of something bigger than himself;**
- **Leigh looking out, alone, over the sea from a cliff-top, calling this the best moment of his life;**
- **Derek, a teacher, who described how looking down, as a child, into rock-pools enabled him to imagine worlds beyond his own experience, so influencing his beliefs about the universe and decision to be a biologist;**
- **A whole school gathered to mourn the death in a fire, of a pupil, and her older brother, remembering her life through readings, prayer and silence.**

An understanding of spiritual development requires more than just a collection of examples. Exploring how the key questions in the next five sections apply to children will reveal distinctive features of spiritual development, even if you reach conclusions different from mine. Your responses will depend on your own understanding of spiritual development and yourself.

Is spiritual the same as religious development?

While there is a strong historical link between spiritual development and religion, a growing consensus agrees with Her Majesty's Inspectorate (DES, 1985, p32) that *religious education ... is contained within this area but is not identical with it.* As Ofsted (1994, p 8) stated, *'spiritual' is not synonymous with 'religious'; all areas of the curriculum may contribute to pupils' spiritual development.*

Smith (1999), from a Christian perspective, distinguishes between two main usages of 'spiritual' as:

- **an essential aspect of being human; and**
- **a term implying judgments of approval or disapproval.**

The first shows it to be common to everyone. We return to the implications of the second shortly.

Membership of a faith community usually requires that one subscribes to specific beliefs or practices. Spirituality is often viewed as more of a personal response, though many religious traditions – including Catholics, Jews and Muslims – see beliefs and spirituality as inseparable. However, schoolteachers have a responsibility to meet all children's needs in relation to spiritual development. As most children are not members of a faith community, how can their spiritual development depend on such an affiliation? This calls for an inclusive understanding – meaning that it takes account of all children – although it may be linked to religious faith, and faith communities may provide especially good environments. As Wright (2000, p96) says, *what is needed is a pedagogy capable of addressing both the universality of humanity's spiritual aspirations and the actuality of distinct spiritual traditions.*

Spiritual development may be distinguished from belief in that this involves:

- **types of experiences, like those above; and**
- **types of questions, involving a search for self-understanding.**

These types of questions fall into three main groups.

- **Who am I?**
- **Where do I fit in?**
- **Why am I here?**

These are existential questions about our identity, place and purpose within the wider scheme of things, which relate to all people, regardless of age, background, culture or religion. These factors influence how we answer these questions, but spiritual development is concerned with what is most important about ourselves as people, as Wright's (2000, p104) definition suggests:

> *spirituality is the relationship of the individual, within community and tradition, to that which is – or is perceived to be – of ultimate concern, ultimate value, and ultimate truth, as appropriated through an informed, sensitive and reflective striving for spiritual wisdom.*

The question 'Who am I?' seems, initially, to be simply a matter of individual identity. However, a little thought shows that this is related to 'Where do I fit in?' because we all have multiple identities. Think and note down some of the identities that you have. This might include specific roles such as parent, partner, child, member of a choir, trainee teacher, expert cook, poor speller, obsessive rock-climber… How you see yourself, and how others see you, varies depending on the context. For instance, how I behave and see myself is quite different when I am with my mother than when I am playing sport, trying to mend a broken toilet or teaching a new class of children. Cupitt (1991) argues that we create meaning by constructing coherent personal narratives and that we all, throughout life, constantly tell new, increasingly accurate, stories to explain our experience. Enhancing spiritual development may be seen as, in part, helping children to create increasingly coherent personal narratives about themselves.

Hay with Nye (1998) describe children's spiritual development as involving what they call 'relational consciousness', which may be seen as comprising four 'layers':

- **child/self;**
- **child/other people;**
- **child/world;**
- **child/God (or a Transcendent Other).**

Tiny infants are literally working out the difference between themselves and other people, the relationship between their body and what is 'other'. Young children go on to explore their relationships with other people, the world around them and what is transcendent or beyond. We become who we are through the relationships we form. In Hull's words (1998, p66), *spirituality exists not inside people, but between them*. We are not independent so much as interdependent. This helps explain how different parts of the world and the environment are linked and affect each other. Hay and Nye's description recognises that people search for a relationship with the transcendent, beyond the world we can perceive, while leaving it open whether this is described as God. It seems as if all people struggle, at some time, with the question 'why are we here?', though we may come to different answers. Most of the time, we do not think about such questions in depth, but they surface at different points in our lives and can never be conclusively answered.

Points for consideration and discussion

Do you think that these sorts of questions are relevant to young children?

What do children gain from 'awe and wonder' experiences?

What might transcendence mean other than experience of God, or an out-of-body experience?

At what points are people especially open to the 'why' questions?

Is spirituality just about exotic or strange experiences, or opportunities for 'awe and wonder'?

You may associate spirituality with out-of-body experiences, new age spirituality or moving to a different state of consciousness or awareness. Some people believe in a spiritual world entirely separate from the material world. The importance of 'transcendence' – going beyond the limits of normal experience or understanding – has a long history in religious and other traditions. However, an inclusive approach must root children's spiritual development in everyday experience, rather than what is special, or out-of-the-ordinary.

Ofsted (2004, p13) rightly emphasises the need for children to develop an appreciation of 'mystery, paradox and ambiguity'. Spiritual development involves experience, and acceptance of, what is mysterious and not capable of being fully understood.

Openness to this and acceptance of inconclusive answers may come more naturally to young children, as the world is more puzzling and mysterious for them than for adults.

Wright (2000, p42) describes relational consciousness as *involving an unusual level of consciousness or perceptiveness*. Spiritual development seems to involve an awareness of something 'beyond the apparent' in:

- **one's own and other people's feelings and actions, leading to greater emotional awareness and insight; or**
- **one's own place in something larger, bringing a changed sense of perspective.**

Many teachers associate spiritual development primarily with 'awe and wonder' experiences. While a raging sea, a great musical performance or the night sky may affect us profoundly, pause to think why. This helps one gain, or re-gain, perspective, by reducing one's concentration on oneself and immediate gratification. Authentic spiritual experience goes beyond simply making ourselves calmer or more relaxed, valuable though that may be, into understanding how others feel and one's place as part of something bigger.

Is spiritual development only about what makes people feel good?

Spirituality is often seen as a solitary, emotional, interior activity, separate from considerations of value, where only one's own concerns matter and where one can retreat from what is difficult. Smith writes (1999, p3), disapprovingly, that *a great deal of discussion of spiritual development seems to inhabit a rosy world where everything is beautiful*. The most overlooked and difficult aspect of spiritual development is that the search for answers to 'Who am I?' and 'Where do I fit in?' brings even young children — and their teachers — up against painful and potentially painful questions.

I asked you to consider 'at what points are people especially open to "why" questions?' This seems to happen frequently at life-changing, often difficult or wonderful, times. My father's death was significant in prompting these questions for me. Several teachers in my research cited the birth of their own children. Others spoke of how the illness of a pupil prompted a deeper level of questioning and of empathy. The tragic death of the little girl I mentioned earlier led, I believe, to a profound spiritual experience for our school community. Other examples include the start, or the break-up, of significant relationships, or major disasters such as the attack on the Twin Towers on 11 September 2001 or the 2004 tsunami. You will be able to think of others for yourself.

Although many adults find this difficult, the search for meaning also involves how we, ourselves, make sense of painful, and potentially painful, experiences and how we help children to do so. This raises two questions.

- **Do young children worry about painful, and potentially painful, experiences?**
- **Shouldn't we protect children, especially very young ones, from thinking about them?**

As soon as one asks the first question, the answer becomes clear. We have all seen how small children move rapidly from joy to frustration and back again. Greenfield (2000, pp51–2) indicates that young children experience emotion more intensely than adults. There is no reason to suppose that children do not experience painful and potentially painful emotions, as well as great joy, albeit for a shorter time. Children do seek answers to questions such as these.

- **Will my mother still love me when I do something wrong?**
- **What has happened to people, or pets, who are no longer here?**
- **Who made the world?**

How this is expressed will vary with age and with young children's limited experience of language, so that they may use play or drawing rather than words. If you don't believe me, watch and listen out for whether, and how, children express such concerns, especially when they think they are not observed.

Whether we should protect young children from thinking about painful or potentially painful questions is harder. Adults have a responsibility to protect children from certain influences – such as excessive violence or inappropriate sexual images – though 'excessive' and 'inappropriate' immediately indicate a need for judgment. Children, especially in Key Stage 2, are far more street-wise and aware of these (not least from watching television) than adults think. We can pretend that a nasty world out there doesn't exist, but for many children it is a reality and all will find out about it at some time.

Learning involves trying to make sense of experience of which one's understanding is only partial. Where adults enable and encourage children to raise difficult questions and are prepared to respond honestly, while keeping open the possibility of further search, this helps children make sense of them. Of course, a four-year-old child is likely to need a different response from that given to a seven- or an eleven-year-old child. What matters is that children are helped to make sense of the questions at their own level – which requires adults to attend to those questions.

This is not easy. Many adults tend to discourage difficult questions, are reluctant to answer them or offer answers which stop the child's exploration. There are several reasons for this. Some are mundane, such as lack of time or the wish not to be interrupted. Sometimes, teachers are, rightly, wary of offering answers which may conflict with the cultural, religious and other beliefs which children bring from home, especially when these involve very definite answers. However, adults often think that they *should* have conclusive answers, rather than help the child to keep wondering. Sometimes, such questions trigger memories and reactions which are distressing, or at least, uncomfortable. For example, in my research, one teacher made comments that indicated negative feelings about her own education. From then on, she made so many excuses why it was inconvenient to visit that I had to abandon my research there. I think that I had, unintentionally, awakened some memories which she did not wish to face.

Points for consideration and discussion

Should young children be encouraged to ask questions about whatever they are worried about?

Would you welcome these sorts of questions in a class discussion?

How do you respond to questions that you are reluctant to answer?

How is spiritual development linked to values?

I mentioned Smith's view that 'spiritual' implies judgments of approval or disapproval, or what is valued. 'Values' often denote rather vague, soft-centred statements of principles. But in Eaude (2004, p2) I quote Halstead and Taylor's view that values are *principles and fundamental convictions, ... beliefs, ... ideals, ... and standards* which guide one's behaviour. Spiritual development is intimately connected with values because these both reflect and structure the sort of person one is or becomes.

Values both indicate our priorities and influence our actions. For instance, spending money on private schooling or home improvements, on foreign holidays or giving to charity, reflect different sets of values, as does spending leisure time watching television or playing with one's children. When an elderly parent requires a high level of care, adult children often have to decide whether or not to sacrifice something that they hold dear, such as career opportunities, privacy or money. More mundanely, things as simple as what you value most – for example your reputation, your appearance or your achievements – tell others a great deal about yourself. So, the decisions we make throughout life depend on our values, with different values sometimes conflicting. Much of the time, we do not have to face such decisions, but our values become most evident when difficult choices have to be made.

Spiritual development should not be seen as primarily about an internal, individual and value-free process. Think whether there is such a thing as negative spirituality. An extreme example is Adolf Hitler. He was a compelling speaker, with a strong set of beliefs and a clear sense both of who he was and of his role. Although these characteristics are often called spiritual, few would see him as spiritually developed, whether because of his egocentricity, his inflexibility or his cruelty. Less extremely, calling the use of drugs or mind-altering experiences 'spiritual' easily leads to escapism, rather than providing an authentic answer to the 'who am I?', 'where do I fit in?' and 'why am I here?' questions.

Hull (1996) argues that the vagueness of how 'spirituality' is used obscures conflict about values and tends towards a self-indulgent and uncritical acceptance of individualistic values. Values are never simply individual, for they are always located within a cultural setting, in the case of Western society based strongly on money and consumption. Much as we may talk of people worshipping a pop star or a football team, a culture's spirituality is evident in what it most values. Ultimately, therefore, judgments of what is worthwhile must underpin authentic spiritual development.

Hull sees one central role of education as enabling young people to be critical of inauthentic and transient values. While this process is most often associated with adolescents overtly exploring and asserting their own identity, younger children can be helped to search, question and reflect on what matters most to them and not to accept other people's values and beliefs uncritically.

The media and advertising provide sophisticated, subtle and usually very attractive messages, based on values which encourage consumerism and consumption: that what you own, what you wear or how you look defines who you are, a message strongly reinforced by the peer group. It is no wonder that children find these glitzy values more appealing than those presented at home and school.

Let us consider the implications for young children. Values are shaped to a large extent by the family background, with a wide range of other influences, from local community to school, from sports club to faith community, from TV to peer group. All provide messages about what is significant. Passionate support for one particular football team may form part of some children's values. Different cultural traditions – for example, how girls, especially, from Muslim backgrounds are brought up to value modesty, particularly in dress – may emphasise values that are unfamiliar to others, or to you.

Each child inherits a framework of values, but has to internalise his or her own values – that is work out, think through, and make these his or her own. Challenging a child's values may easily be seen as disrespectful or be counter-productive, especially as children approach adolescence. We all know how attractive it is to do what those in authority disapprove of. So, teachers face two potentially difficult tensions:

- **being respectful of different cultural and religious traditions, while helping children not to accept these uncritically;**
- **wishing to pass on one's own values, while recognising that children need to work out their own.**

In Chapter 10, I suggest that who you are as a teacher cannot be dissociated from who you are as a person. The values that you bring to the classroom influence children, often subtly, at least as much as what you teach directly. How you relate to other people, how you create appropriate expectations, how you live, the values which you espouse, rubs off on children, whether you like it or not. Remember that Standard 1, called *'professional values and practice'* includes:

- **high expectations (S1.1);**
- **respect and consideration (S1.2); and**
- **demonstrating and promoting positive values, attitudes and behaviour (S1.3).**

Is spiritual *development* the right word to use in relation to children?

Many religious traditions, especially within Christianity, suggest that adults have much to learn from children in terms of spiritual experience and qualities. For example, Jesus said *Anyone who does not welcome the kingdom of God like a little child will never enter it*. (St Mark, Chapter 10, verse 15). The theologian Rahner described children as fully human creatures worthy of dignity and respect and as models for adults.

Points for consideration and discussion

Which qualities related to spiritual development do children have and we, as adults, lose or suppress?

What tends to make adults lose or suppress these?

How, if at all, can we, as adults, learn to rediscover these qualities?

You may have moved from not knowing what spiritual development was all about to dreading it. But remember that children have wonderful qualities, the more so the younger they are. Among these are: openness; curiosity; a capacity for joy; and an ability to live in, and enjoy, the here-and-now.

Young children can show remarkable sensitivity and empathy for other people and, at times, show these in extraordinary ways. For instance, one teacher described to me recently how two young children had, unprompted, gently stroked a severely disabled child, integrated in a mainstream class, when he was very distressed during the performance of a play. Often, busy-ness, embarrassment, or concern for status or power seem to inhibit adults from exhibiting these qualities.

Priestley (2000) points out how poorly the metaphor of *development* reflects the profound capacity of young children for spiritual experience. The idea of development is drawn from a theory of learning based on the ideas of Jean Piaget, an immensely influential psychologist, *in which the child is represented as accumulating skills in stages, each set of which is incorporated and enlarged by the further skills acquired in the subsequent stages. The adult is thus seen as an elaboration of all the capacities which are simply embryonic in childhood.* (Egan, 1999, p86). Whatever language we use tends to presuppose a particular view. Different metaphors, such as *journey* or *growth*, are more dynamic and capture the idea of search. While this may seem rather an academic argument, different language can help us think in new and creative ways about what spiritual development involves. However, despite the limitations of the term 'development', its use in legislation and the Ofsted Framework means that we are to some extent stuck with it.

You will be familiar with the term IQ (intelligence quotient), claimed to be a measure of intellectual ability, and perhaps EQ or emotional intelligence, as the ability to regulate emotions and behaviour. Zohar and Marshall (2001) introduce SQ as a measure of spiritual intelligence. While an interesting idea, it leads the authors into presenting spiritual development as something that can be measured, with techniques that can be learnt to raise SQ levels. I find SQ an unhelpful, over-hierarchical way of thinking of children's spiritual experience.

Fisher (1998) has devised a measure of children's spiritual 'health', based on quantifiable measures. Many of these concern children's relationship to God, though they also draw on the range of relationships highlighted by Hay with Nye. While, again, I find quantifying this unhelpful, the metaphor of health helps to reflect that this fluctuates, affected by both internal resources and external factors.

What is spiritual experience?

It is valuable to distinguish between the child's experience and the provision which a school, or a teacher, makes: rather like that between learning and teaching. What really matters is how and what children learn. We hope that our teaching enhances learning, but we can never be sure. Good provision for spiritual development seeks to enhance important but elusive types of experience and qualities. Consider, for example, Ofsted's (1995, p82) guidance to inspectors on judging provision for spiritual development:

> judgments ... should be based on the extent to which the school provides its pupils with knowledge and insight into values and beliefs and enables them to reflect on their experiences in a way that develops their spiritual awareness and self-knowledge.

My own research, summarised in Eaude (2003), led to the following definition (though no definition is completely adequate):

> spiritual experience is that which enables, or enhances, greater personal integration within a framework of relationships by fostering exploration, conscious and otherwise, of identity and purpose, transcending the current level of self-knowledge and altering, or regaining, appropriate perspectives and values.

This tries to be inclusive, based on the types of experience and response that help the child – or anyone – make sense of the big, difficult questions of life. The two key practical questions, considered in the second half of the book, are: where, and how, children's spiritual (and moral, social or cultural) experience 'happens'; how to make provision conducive to such experience.

We are jumping ahead of ourselves, but let me highlight a paradox that such an experience can happen anywhere, and at any time, but will not necessarily happen because of any particular provision or range of experiences, yet we can create environments and encourage experiences which make it more likely.

So, we have to steer a course between thinking that such experience will happen automatically and imagining that spiritual development only takes place during activities specifically set up for that purpose.

In considering provision to encourage SMSC, we shall look at:

- **the features of an enabling ethos and environment;**
- **how particular opportunities arise in different subject areas. HMI (DES, 1985, paragraph 78, p32) were surely right that** dance, drama, music, art and literature witness to the element of mystery in human experience across the centuries and in every culture, but ... few parts of the curriculum ... do not in some way show that influence;
- **the difficulty of planning for what is unpredictable and assessing outcomes which are often unclear and rarely measurable.**

I indicated that this chapter would be challenging and that spiritual development does not lend itself to definitions. I have offered you three definitions, none entirely satisfactory, but all helping to illuminate what spiritual development is about. Before we turn to moral, social and cultural development, consider the following points, as they are relevant, with slight variation, to each of the four elements of SMSC.

Points for consideration and discussion

Which values do you bring as a person to your role as a teacher?

How do you demonstrate these in your teaching?

What values commonly seen in society do you disapprove of and do you 'deal with' these with children?

Recommended reading

Eaude, T (2003) *New Perspectives on Spiritual Development.* Birmingham: National Primary Trust: *A short summary, written for a teacher audience, of my own research.*

Hay, D with Nye, R (1998) *The Spirit of the Child.* London: Fount. Probably the most influential and accessible book on young children's spirituality.

Smith, D (1999) *Making sense of Spiritual Development.* Nottingham: The Stapleford Centre. A very useful pamphlet that approaches spiritual development from a Christian perspective, in an inclusive and thoughtful way.

Other references

Carr, D (1995) Towards a Distinctive Conception of Spiritual Education *Oxford Review of Education.* 21, no. 1, pp83–98

Cupitt, D (1991) *What is a Story?* London: SCM Press

DES (1985) *The curriculum from 5 to 16 (Curriculum Matters 2).*

Eaude, T (2004) *Values Education – developing positive attitudes.* Birmingham: National Primary Trust

Egan, K (1999) *Children's minds, talking rabbits and clockwork oranges.* New York: Teachers College Press

Fisher, J (1998) *Helps and Hindrances to Fostering Students' Spiritual Health.* Unpublished paper at the Roehampton Conference

Greenfield, S (2001) *The Private Life of the Brain.* London: Penguin

Hull, J (1996) The Ambiguity of Spiritual Values pp33–44, in Halstead, JM and Taylor, MJ (eds) *Values in Education and Education in Values.* London: Falmer

Ofsted (1994) *Spiritual, Moral, Social and Cultural Development*

Ofsted (1995) *Guidance on the Inspection of Nursery and Primary Schools.*

Priestley, J (2000) Moral and Spiritual growth pp113–28, in J Mills and R Mills (eds) *Childhood Studies – a reader in perspectives of childhood.* London: Routledge

Wright A (2000) *Spirituality and Education.* London: RoutledgeFalmer

Zohar, D and Marshall, I (2001) *Spiritual Intelligence – the Ultimate Intelligence.* London: Bloomsbury

3 WHAT DOES MORAL DEVELOPMENT INVOLVE?

By the end of this chapter you should:

- **have explored and broadened your understanding of moral development;**
- **understand why children are often confused about how they should act;**
- **see the importance of habituation, example and structure;**
- **have thought about the role of expectations, rewards and rules;**
- **realise that every aspect of school life affects moral development.**

This will help you to meet Standards:
➔ *S 1.1, 1.2, 1.3, 2.4, 2.7, 3.3.9, 3.3.14*

Since the moral domain – that of action – and the social domain – that of interaction – are closely linked, this chapter and the next cover areas which overlap. The relationships we form influence how we act and our actions take place within, and are affected by, social contexts. Ofsted (1995, p82) states that [inspectors'] judgments should be based on the extent to which the school *teaches the principles which distinguish right from wrong.* If only moral development were so easy. However, Ofsted (1995, p84) recognises that *the essence of moral development is to build a framework of values which regulate personal behaviour through principles rather than through fear of punishment or reward.* Moral development is something much wider, and more profound, than behaviour management. I shall suggest that a subtle mixture of example, habituation and conscious choice helps children build up the qualities that make up their character and sense of self, as a basis for appropriate action.

Points for consideration and discussion

What are the potential problems with Ofsted's definition?

What do you believe to be the most powerful influences on how children act?

Why do some children find it so hard to act appropriately?

All generations of adults complain that the young lack a sense of morality, and that standards of behaviour have declined. Children's behaviour is almost certainly one of your main concerns. It is what frustrates me most as a teacher. Bad behaviour can disrupt a really well-planned lesson. Just one child's behaviour can undermine any teacher's confidence. The behaviour of a difficult class can, over time, make life very hard, and create a climate where all children's learning is disrupted. However, the Steer report (2005, p6) cites Ofsted's judgment that behaviour is excellent or good in 92 per cent of primary schools. Most children in most schools behave well most of the time, look after each other and do not end up acting antisocially.

One reason why teachers worry so much about behaviour is that children, especially as a group, can provoke emotional responses we find hard to regulate. By an unconscious process called projection, we may feel anxiety or fear – or more positive emotions – as a result of someone else feeling this. Kimes Myers (1997, p8) draws on Erikson's work that the adult–child relationship is not a one-way process, describing it as 'cogwheeling'. She writes *when we engage in relationships with young children ... the child within us also has a developing edge.* This sort of response can result in a situation like the following.

Case study

A terrible way to deal with bad behaviour – and a lucky escape

In a particularly difficult class of ten year olds, Danny kept reading a football comic in class, ignoring several requests to put it away. I became exasperated and eventually threatened to take it and tear it up if he persisted. Having made that threat, I felt obliged to carry it out when he carried on. He said he would bring his dad, whom I knew to be a rough character, to see me after school. Sure enough, he did. The only thing I did right in the whole incident was to apologise. I was lucky because, although Danny's father was initially angry, he gave his son a good telling-off for not doing what his teacher said. A good example of a parent being consistent in supporting the teacher and a lesson for me not to respond to provocation by allowing myself to be provoked.

What is the basis of moral development?

Think about what influences your actions. It may help to categorise them like this:

Your background	Your values and beliefs	The specific context

Separating those in the first two columns is difficult. Those in the left-hand column are likely to include your family background, your school, groups such as the Brownies, a sports club or a faith community. These will have influenced what is in the middle column, maybe that you should always help anyone in trouble, or each for him or herself, or whatever will make you happy. Early influences exerted by parents, by other significant individuals and the wider culture remains strong, even when we rebel against them. Our values and beliefs, usually made explicit during adolescence, provide a structure for how we act, but, in practice, our actions always occur within, and are influenced by, a specific context. We all act differently with our parents, with our friends, or on our own; or when driving a car, shopping or in the shower.

Many people argue that morality is based in religion and that moral decline stems from a lack of religious belief to provide a set of values and principles on which to base one's behaviour. Even 30 years ago, there was widespread acceptance of Christianity forming a common basis for morality. This is much harder to sustain now. It is open to debate whether or not religious belief is a good thing, but there are now many more, often conflicting, sources that influence values and attitudes, and an uncertainty within society about what comes within the scope of morality. As White (in Smith and Standish, 1997, p19) suggests, *the problem is not moral decline, but a certain lack of confidence about how we should behave and what we should believe.*

A framework of religious belief remains, for many people, a powerful moral influence. Although religion − usually the Judaeo-Christian tradition − may influence most people's morality in the West, there are plenty of examples of moral codes and good people who do not base their morality in religion. Since children come from families and backgrounds with widely different beliefs, expectations and aspirations, teachers can no longer assume that children's values are grounded in faith, or in any particular faith. Religion and morality are no longer necessarily linked. If you teach in a school with a Christian foundation the school's mission will probably be based on moral principles explicitly related to Christianity. But, even there, many other influences impact on moral development. In part, children are confused because society is less sure of itself. Children grow up in an increasingly fragmented and confusing social and cultural climate, often including that of the family.

Perhaps the greatest source of confusion is that of society beyond the school and the family. Schools reflect, and are influenced by, the wider society they serve. Children are bombarded with messages from sources such as television, the internet, magazines and advertising. These affect children both consciously and at deeper levels, by being carefully crafted to appeal to them, using very sophisticated methods, especially visual imagery. Their aims are far from neutral; they are often designed to encourage children buy particular products and, cumulatively, they give out the message that fulfilment depends on how you look and what you own. The values of a society heavily focused on consumption and commodities add to young children's confusion about how they should act and what they should strive for.

The peer group is influential both in reinforcing these messages and at a more immediate level of individual choice, most obviously in terms of group identity with children as they approach and enter adolescence. However, Lloyd and Duveen (1992), for instance, discuss how the gender identity of children as young as four and five is influenced by the peer group; and Renold (2004) shows how intense the pressure to conform can be for older boys who exhibit non-typical boys' behaviour. While the pressure to be part of the in-group has always been strong, the powerful, informal influences outlined above have made this even stronger. While the school or class ethos can help counter these, the looser structure of the playground is often much harder for the often vulnerable children who are tempted to imitate those whose misbehaviour is attractive.

These may be seen as external influences. However, the basis of moral and social development is how children have been, and are, treated in their own family and home background. Early relationships with, and feedback from, significant adults influence profoundly how babies understand themselves and learn to regulate their emotional responses. Long before conscious thought happens, children learn by watching, by responding. Even accepting Kagan's (1994) case that each of us is predisposed to a certain way of responding, early feedback from carers determines how children learn to regulate their responses. As Gerhardt (2004, p24) writes, *unconsciously acquired, non-verbal patterns and expectations … are inscribed in the brain outside conscious awareness, in the period of infancy and … underpin our behaviour in relationships through life*. Secure relationships and reinforcement of appropriate responses helps to 'hard-wire' these patterns. Even then, intense anxiety may result in aggressive or withdrawn behaviour. We consider this further in looking at social development.

How do children learn in the moral domain?

Put simply, how we make sense of the world, at any time, involves a set of patterns of understanding or, more accurately, many of these. Learning takes place when new experience, providing feedback to the brain, unsettles this homeostasis. This may take many forms:

- **sensory, such as pain;**
- **emotional, such as a gesture of support;**
- **moral, such as a sign of approval or otherwise.**

Such feedback may reinforce or alter the previous understanding, so that a new homeostasis is formed, with this process constantly recurring.

Many presuppositions about teaching are based on the belief (often unconscious) that learning is always an explicit, conscious process. Much of our learning precedes, or bypasses, language and consciousness, for example by modelling and through visual images from TV and advertising. Bruner describes three modes of learning, the **enactive**, the **iconic** and the **symbolic** (including language), simply described in the website cited in the references. Enactive learning, through, for instance, touch or mimicry, and iconic learning, through images, is evident from very early childhood, well before symbolic thinking appears. While the symbolic can be seen as the 'highest' of these three modes, these are not consecutive stages and adults continue to learn using all three modes. Young children learn mainly through enactive and iconic modes. However, throughout life, the profoundest lessons are learnt through these modes. For example, our emotional responses often seem to precede, and be largely impervious to, the influence of conscious choice and thought. Or learning something really difficult depends on seeing and doing as well as listening.

Bateson, a biologist and anthropologist, distinguishes between two sorts of feedback, using the analogy of shooting a gun. When shooting at a fixed target, you can correct your aim slightly on the second and subsequent shots. However, when shooting at a moving target such as a flying bird, the process is less deliberate and one cannot make small corrections. Instead, one has to repeat the whole movement, with adaptations, for the next shot. The latter depends on experiencing the movement as a whole, the former more like a process of conscious reflection which can be repeated with small adjustments.

The example of shooting at a flying bird shows the importance of learning by watching and copying. The younger the child, the more powerful an influence example tends to be, not simply because they are impressionable but because they rely less on conscious symbolic learning. Even when children are older, they learn more by what they see than by what they hear. Think of the influence of David Beckham or Kelly Holmes and how children look up to them. The model, or example, provided by adults, for good or ill, is more influential than what they say. Words can reinforce this, but without a good example they have only a limited impact. One mother pleaded with me as a headteacher to wear a helmet when I rode my bike, as otherwise she could not persuade her sons to do so. She was right. How parents and teachers act influences children's actions, like it or not.

Points for consideration and discussion

What is the basis of why you act morally? (When you do!)

What was the most important influence in learning to do so?

Which adults have most helped you to become who you are? And how?

Do children learn by habit or conscious choice?

Most discussion about moral development concentrates on conscious, deliberate actions, rather like adjusting one's sights to hit a fixed target. Kohlberg (1987) describes a hierarchy with six stages, suggesting that, as people reflect on the consequences of previous actions, they adopt appropriate courses of action, gradually refining their choices, moving towards independent, rational choice. This model, while helpful, is open to two main criticisms, that it:

- **is based on an assumption of morality having (broadly) the same end point for everyone;**
- **overemphasises the role of conscious choice.**

Gilligan (1982) suggested that gender may affect significantly one's view of what moral development is about. So, girls may see relationship as more important than justice, interdependence more than autonomy. A similar challenge could be made from the perspective of different cultures, as different cultures or communities may prioritise diverse qualities. The end point of moral development cannot be taken for granted and is certainly not just about being able to talk about what one should do, but acting appropriately – often referred to as 'walking the talk'.

Oakeshott (as discussed in Erricker and Erricker, 2000, pp98–102) highlights that moral education must encourage correct action out of both habit and the reflective application of moral criteria.

Both are important if children are to internalise their values, which provide a framework to guide their actions when acting autonomously.

The word 'habit' has the negative connotation of doing something like an automaton, without thinking. Yet most moral actions bypass, or are hardly influenced by, conscious thought, as a result of habituation, as if immersed in a particular way of acting. This is rather like learning a new language by listening to, and speaking, it all the time. The reason why I do not attack vulnerable old ladies or steal expensive cars is only occasionally brought to consciousness. Most children are kind to each other because 'that is the way we treat each other here'. So, one key aspect of moral development is how children can learn to act appropriately, by habit, so that it becomes 'second-nature', similar to what sports coaches call 'muscle memory'. Given that children learn especially through enactive and iconic modes, moral development depends on the examples that they see and the practice of acting appropriately.

However, moral development also involves working out how to act when different values and principles clash. For example, how does one balance honesty and loyalty when a friend asks if you like something they're proud of, but which you can't stand? When is it right not to obey rules? This requires an ability to reflect critically on several factors, and weigh them against each other. This is hard for anyone, but especially for young children, where much of the language of morality is abstract and difficult to understand. If children are only offered simple solutions, or discussion does not go beyond caring and kindness, they may not be equipped to resolve such conflicts or to work out what to do in unfamiliar contexts. Children need to reflect, especially in Key Stage 2, on the consequences of their actions and whether they will lead to the sort of outcomes they wish to achieve. The vocabulary to help them reflect critically and an ability to engage with complexity are largely developed through discussion, over time, of what they did and might have done differently.

What can adults do to influence moral development?

Expecting teachers to 'teach children right from wrong' is simplistic. Almost all children have a sense of fairness deeply ingrained. Think how often they will complain that a decision is not fair. Similarly, most children know that they should not steal or lie and that they should treat other people well. It is rather that the confusion discussed above makes it hard to know what to do and to act on this. Perhaps, the hardest lesson in moral development is that, ultimately, adults need to relinquish control. The key task is to equip children with the qualities and deep-rooted motivations to enable them to become the people they would wish to be.

Our motives for action, whether good or bad, are of two sorts, extrinsic or intrinsic. Extrinsic motivation comes from outside, such as tangible reward or punishment. Intrinsic motivation is because the action is worthwhile in itself, or the reward or punishment are more intangible, such as approval or loss of prestige. Moral development involves trying to ensure that motivation becomes intrinsic rather than only because of external consequences. Moral development involves children internalising their motivation for action rather than simply being compliant.

For example, Family Links, a programme to encourage emotional literacy, emphasises the importance of children making choices and being aware of their consequences using the idea of personal power. This enables children to be actively responsible for their actions, within an environment that provides nurture and support. It can also help to separate who children are from what they do, to avoid fragile identities becoming even more fragile, recognising that some children's experience makes it hard for them to exercise such choice without a great deal of adult support. For adults to be too direct or controlling is likely to prove counter-productive. Often, we need to work subtly, through the unconscious, by affirmation of the positive, by example, by telling stories. So, the environment created is, as we shall see further in Chapter 7, central to how adults can support children's moral development.

Let us think about rewards and rules. Rewards may be tangible, such as money or a new bike, or symbolic, such as a certificate or a warning to represent approval or otherwise. Stickers or certificates for good behaviour can make explicit adult expectations and reinforce positive behaviour. They can help children to get into good habits in the short term, but an approach based on tangible rewards, even when effective, tends to have a limited shelf-life, especially when they are handed out too freely. It rarely operates successfully as a long-term strategy, especially for those whose behaviour it is most intended to influence. More importantly, an approach where the prime motivation is extrinsic tends to work only while the reward remains in place. A classic example is that 'bribes' to work hard or achieve success make good behaviour dependent on the reward, so discouraging intrinsic motivation.

Rules form an important part of a framework for moral development, in making clear what is expected. However, too great an emphasis on rules can lead children's actions depending too much on external reward or punishment. Paradoxically, children need both to operate within a framework of rules but learn to see the reasoning behind them, so that they internalise why they matter. So, encouraging reflection and discussion on the reasons behind rules, or developing them together, helps to avoid children being overtly compliant but flouting the rules whenever possible. This may not matter with petty regulations, but in terms of values children have to internalise how to act for themselves. The best rules are there to guide, not to confine. As with cooking to a recipe or following instructions without understanding what you are trying to assemble, you are lost when the context changes. Think how too strict a regime leads adolescents to reject the whole structure imposed by parents, a community or a religion.

What is a moral community?

It may help to see the school and the classroom as moral communities with a tradition of values. Some values are made explicit in a mission statement or policies, such as the school's religious foundation, or beliefs about equal opportunities, or role in the community. But the most important, such as what achievements we value, how inclusive we are, how we deal with difference and how we relate to each other, are implicit in our actions – the true litmus test of moral development.

We tend to have a narrow view of moral development, seeing it as a bolt-on, like an additional subject, rather than integral to every aspect of school life, extending into all areas of the curriculum. Jackson et al. (1993) researched the moral life of American schools by observing and discussing the whole range of school life. This included the moral instruction in specific lessons and within ordinary lessons, rituals such as assemblies and how children were welcomed, rules and visual displays. They argue that teachers' comments in the ordinary life of the classroom and reactions of approval or disapproval indicate moral judgments. I shall never forget how one teacher threw a finished piece of work straight into the fire when shown it by the only boy in the class who was (just) worse at woodwork than me. Moreover, whatever is valued or otherwise, the curriculum organisation, how children are spoken to and how the furniture is arranged, have embedded within them moral connotations. Since teachers' actions cannot be value-neutral, any approach to education is underpinned by moral beliefs. Indeed, education is a moral enterprise, with schools often the nearest that many children get to an experience of a moral community.

Points for consideration and discussion

How is moral development different from managing behaviour?

What are the advantages and disadvantages of stickers and rewards?

What do you understand by the term 'moral community'?

The teacher's role in moral development is much harder when children have experienced, and often continue to experience, overlapping, sometimes conflicting, frameworks of expectation and response. One major source of confusion comes when children experience different value systems at home and at school. Many parents are confused about what expectations to have of their children and how to back these up. The most obvious is when children are told by a parent to hit back when someone hits them and the school says otherwise. This is a source of potential conflict with the parent, but the child is torn between two conflicting approaches. In a similar, but less obvious way, different expectations at home and school, for instance on what food to eat or how to dress, as a result of a religious upbringing, can lead to children being asked to make choices not just about that specific course of action but something bigger – which side to take.

Case study

Who runs this school?

Sam was a five year old with a background of terrible abuse and neglect. As soon as he started school, he needed a great deal of support. Despite a wonderful teacher, he was always in trouble, often hit other children and showed little remorse. When asked by a behaviour support teacher to think of a bad name to call other children, he started with one not printable in a book like this! Despite rewards for good behaviour, punishments for bad behaviour, discussions with his mother, being kept separate from other children, nothing seemed to work. He was clever enough to play adults off against each other. When he was told off for being in the wrong playground, it became clear that his teacher, the deputy, had told him to stay in one playground and he had come to me, as head, to gain permission to go in another. His response when challenged was not to look sheepish, or apologise, but simply to ask 'Who runs this school?'

Successful programmes and teachers focus on, and reinforce, the positive aspects of how children act, to encourage them to act appropriately for the right reason. This process is individual, but it happens within a framework of social and cultural expectations, providing boundaries of acceptability, while allowing exploration and reflection. Secure boundaries act as a cocoon, within which children can experiment, take risks, make mistakes and so internalise their values and develop intrinsic motivation. Appropriate expectations from adults help the child not only to feel secure but to create, and internalise, expectations of him or herself. Without these expectations, children are left confused and unsupported. Most children's need for structure diminishes with age, though adult anxiety may, paradoxically, make the structure even more restrictive. We consider further how expectations and aspirations are linked in Chapter 8.

If you are training to teach very young children, you may think this all rather complicated. Of course, younger children need simpler messages, such as 'share your toys' or 'do to other people what you would like them to do to you', to build up good habits of behaviour which stay with them (or not!) as they get older. Parents do not, for instance, reason with toddlers about going near to a fire. Most parents will have no hesitation in stopping a child from hurting a younger brother or sister. Equally, most teachers will, rightly, tell young children that some actions – such as stealing, hurting other people or lying – are wrong. However, children also need to discuss the consequences of their actions and talk about abstract, often difficult, ideas, such as honesty or thoughtfulness. Giving examples of positive qualities and thinking about the motivations of characters in stories will reinforce what children do right by helping them to reflect on what they do and the consequences for themselves and other people.

What qualities do we wish to develop in children?

The Shorter Oxford English Dictionary's definition of 'moral' starts *of or pertaining to human character and behaviour as good or bad*. The word 'character' is somewhat out of fashion in Britain, though used in the United States and increasingly in business. Our character, or who we become, is created in part by:

- **what we have experienced;**
- **how we perceive ourselves now;**
- **imagining who we might become.**

In enhancing moral development teachers must not discount prior experience, and must work with a child's sense of self, helping children to imagine what they may become and believe that this is possible. In focusing on the sort of person one is, or can become, character emphasises the whole range of personal qualities, motivations and actions, holistically. The philosopher Macintyre (1999) argues that Western societies tend to associate morality with a narrow range of decisions, mostly individual and often based on what one should not do. He argues that this is a very different, and flawed, approach from that adopted by the Ancient Greeks and common until the eighteenth century. Their emphasis was on which virtues and qualities a good man (unfortunately it usually was only men) exhibited and how boys would learn these. Right action is based on virtues which are all interlinked and related to the person's place within society. Morality is social as well as individual.

Considering what qualities to encourage in a child looks easy on the surface, but listing these shows that it is more complex. Try completing this chart:

Intrapersonal qualities	Qualities that bridge the intra- and interpersonal	Interpersonal qualities

Some qualities may be seen as intrapersonal, such as patience or courage, others more interpersonal, such as respect or co-operation, whereas some, such as trust or friendliness, bridge the two. This emphasises the close links between moral and social development, between action and interaction. Similarly, Macintyre (1999, p133) distinguishes between competitive and co-operative, and between individual and social virtues.

Which virtues were emphasised naturally changed over time and between cultures. Greek states were very small and usually homogeneous. They excluded women, non-citizens and slaves in a way we would all find unacceptable. In a warrior state, courage was highly valued. In societies based on Christian belief this declined, with humility, which the Greeks would have despised, and forgiveness becoming more important. Although the virtues emphasised may change according to context, the principle of asking what sort of qualities are to be encouraged remains valid. While words like 'character' and 'virtue' may seem old-fashioned, they help to provide a positive way of considering what qualities, habits and actions we wish to encourage, and helping children to do so.

Points for consideration and discussion

What are the characteristics of a 'morally mature' person?

Which of your own qualities do you think are most important?

How much can, and should, teachers encourage children to adopt different approaches from those seen at home or in society?

The Values Education approach is based on the belief that for children to develop values there is a requirement for both *the practical modelling of what these values entail* and *a vocabulary to understand what they mean and how to apply them in practice*. The following 22 values, said to be universal and not based on any one religion, but common to most, constitute a cycle over almost two years, where one value each month can be displayed, demonstrated and discussed. The commitment of the whole staff and a focus for a whole month on one value, in assemblies, in lessons and around the school helps to concentrate everyone in the school on that value and how to live it in practice. The practice of reflection and stillness is also an integral part of the approach.

Values directory

appreciation	caring	co-operation	courage	hope
freedom	patience	understanding	honesty	love
respect	trust	simplicity	humility	peace
friendship	tolerance	responsibility	quality	unity
	happiness	thoughtfulness		

(in Eaude (2004, p5))

We shall return to whether values are universal. While Values Education does not, any more than other similar programmes, offer a panacea, it provides (with adaptation where appropriate) a simple way to enable children to:

- **see examples of positive behaviour modelled so that they come to understand how abstract terms like 'courage' and 'respect' feel like 'from the inside' and how they influence behaviour;**
- **develop a vocabulary to consider how to reflect on these values and on which is most appropriate to adopt in any given context.**

For a more detailed description of Values Education, and its strengths, see Eaude (2004).

This chapter has emphasised the importance of example and a consistent framework within which children can explore and develop positive qualities. However strict your rules, severe your punishments or generous your rewards, however compelling your stories, you will have little long-term impact unless you act appropriately yourself.

Recommended reading

Eaude, T (2004) *Values Education – developing positive attitudes*. Birmingham: National Primary Trust. A short pamphlet outlining the principles of Values Education and how these have been adopted in nine schools.

Jackson, P W, Boostrom, R E, and Hansen, D T (1993) *The Moral Life of Schools.* San Francisco, CA: Jossey Bass. A little known but readable book, which shows how almost everything that happens in schools contributes to moral education.

Smith, R and Standish, P (1997) *Teaching right and wrong – moral education in the balance.* Stoke on Trent: Trentham Books. A series of essays exposing how oversimplified much of the discussion on moral education has become and which will help you to think more deeply about it.

Other references

Bruner, J starfsfolk.khi.is/solrunb/jbruner.htm.3.htm

Erricker, C and Erricker J (2000) *Reconstructing Religious, Spiritual and Moral Education.* London: RoutledgeFalmer

Gerhardt, S (2004) *Why Love Matters: how affection shapes a baby's brain.* Hove: Routledge

Gilligan, C (1982) *In a Different Voice.* Cambridge, MA: Harvard University Press

Kagan, J (1994) *Galen's Prophecy.* London: Free Association

Kimes Myers, B (1997) *Young Children and Spirituality.* London: Routledge

Kohlberg, L (1987) *Child psychology and childhood education: a cognitive–developmental view.* New York: Longman

Lloyd, B and Duveen, G (1992) *Gender Indentities and Education.* Hemel Hempstead: Harvester Wheatsheaf

Macintyre, A (1999) *After Virtue.* London: Duckworth

Ofsted (1995) *Guidance on the Inspection of Nursery and Primary Schools.*

Renold, E (2004) 'Other boys': negotiating non-hegemonic masculinities in the primary school, in *Gender and Education 16 (2)* pp247– 66

Steer A (2005) *Learning behaviour.* Nottingham: DfES

4 WHAT DOES SOCIAL DEVELOPMENT INVOLVE?

By the end of this chapter you should:

- recognise the link between emotional and social development and how this affects the whole range of children's learning;
- have considered further the influence of different values and expectations at school, in the home and elsewhere;
- understand why social development is difficult for all children and especially hard for some.

This will help you to meet Standards:
→ *S 1.1, 1.2, 1.3, 2.4, 2.7, 3.2.4, 3.3.1, 3.3.9, 3.3.14*

At first sight, 'social' appears the most easily understood of the four elements of SMSC. Many parents, unsure of what spiritual or cultural development involves, would see children learning how to interact with each other and with adults as one main purpose of school. Rightly, teachers of young children concentrate heavily on social and emotional development, seeing it embedded in the whole of school life. However, it merits the same detailed exploration as spiritual, moral and cultural development.

Let us start with two descriptions from Ofsted. The first, from the 1999 inspection handbook (1999, p73) sees social development as designed to *encourage pupils to take responsibility, show initiative and develop an understanding of living in a community*. The *2003 Handbook* (Ofsted, 2003, p57) adds that

> *pupils who are socially aware adjust appropriately and sensitively to a range of social contexts. They relate well to others and work successfully as a member of a team. Older pupils share their views and opinions and work towards trying to reach a sensible solution to problems. They show respect for people, living things, property and the environment.*

As with moral development, these emphasise qualities to be developed. The reference to context highlights the link between social and cultural development.

Points for consideration and discussion

How does early experience affect older children's emotional responses and relationships?

What effect does one's emotional state have on one's ability to learn?

To what extent can young children regulate their emotional responses?

Why are relationships so important?

Understanding the role of emotion is essential in considering moral and social development. Like many people, especially men, I learned to distrust emotion, in both myself and other people. The ideal thinker is supposed to be analytic, calm, detached, dispassionate, unemotional. Yet emotion is fundamental to all brain function and good learners must be able to regulate it. While there is insufficient space here to explore the complicated area of how the functioning of the brain affects emotion and behaviour, it is well worth all teachers, but especially those working in the early years, reading about this. The first two chapters of Gerhardt (2004) provide a good introduction, although, like many such books, this overemphasises the brain's physiology, whereas the key lessons for teachers are that:

- **emotion is a more basic brain function than cognition;**
- **behaviour is influenced by how emotion is regulated;**
- **young children experience emotion with particular intensity, probably because their regulatory mechanisms are not well developed;**
- **how well emotion is regulated depends both on the context and on how 'significant others' are attuned and respond to our needs.**

To see why emotion is so important, and the link with behaviour, we need to consider the relationship between babies and those who care for them. Babies literally explore the boundaries between themselves and their prime-carers, both physical, sensory ones, and mental and emotional ones. Emotion, and how significant adults respond, provides a feedback mechanism to influence how the baby 'makes sense' of sensations and experiences. For example, discomfort may cause the baby to feel anxiety, and to cry. The adult's response may comfort the baby, emotionally or physically, by changing a nappy, and so provide security. This helps the child to learn which responses, or behaviours, lead to a good outcome. So, the development of the personality is, from the start, dependent on relationship.

Bowlby (1965) described how a tiny baby builds a relationship with the prime-carer, almost invariably the mother, as attachment. The prime-carer's response affects how the baby learns to regulate his or her emotion. Consistent, reciprocal responses, attuned to the baby's needs, tend to make this attachment secure, so providing a good basis for personality development, whereas disorganised, resistant or avoidant responses tend to dictate the responses of, and the relationships formed by, the developing child. The pattern of attachment and relationships established in early infancy influences how children learn to regulate emotion. Emotional well-being and socialisation is affected, for better or worse, by the sort of response experienced in a process that is to some extent self-perpetuating. Secure relationships help to develop qualities which children need in order to feel secure. While this pattern can be altered to some extent, it remains very influential in how we regulate our emotions and relate to other people.

Evans (2001, p5) summarises a wide range of research that we cannot stop basic emotional responses — joy, distress, anger, fear, surprise and disgust — from happening, but we can learn to regulate these, and so to alter how they affect us and how we act. He distinguishes between emotion, an immediate response, and mood, an associated but more long-term state. How we respond to basic emotion depends to some extent on our mood, which is affected by our immediate relationships and social environment. Being with friends and people whom we love and trust helps us when we are anxious, and a safe, calm environment – a library or an orderly classroom – makes it easier to regulate emotions and responses more appropriately than a nightclub or a busy playground. So, children are less likely to respond aggressively to the same incident when in a calm mood and more so when anxious or frightened.

Maslow's (1968) hierarchy of needs, pictured below, with the lowest level being the most basic needs, helps to link emotional and social development.

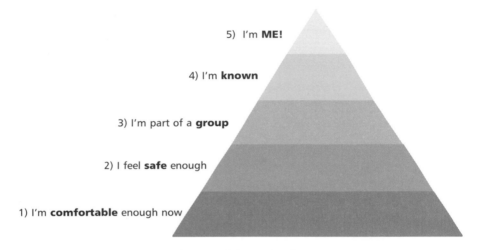

5) I'm **ME!**

4) I'm **known**

3) I'm part of a **group**

2) I feel **safe** enough

1) I'm **comfortable** enough now

Fig. 4.1 Maslow's hierarchy of needs

Maslow describes five levels of needs, with every child and adult needing to:

Level 1: reduce current physical discomforts first: hunger, thirst, pain, air, temperature, smells, balance, noise, light, and rest (sleep). When those are satisfied …

Level 2: try to fill the need to feel safe enough: both the Level 1 discomforts and avoiding danger and insecurity for the next few days and weeks. Then …

Level 3: feel accepted by, and part of, a group of other people, such as family, tribe, group or clan. When the first three levels of need are met, one can then …

Level 4: be known and appreciated and recognised as special and valuable in a group. Only then can one move to …

Level 5: become fully ourselves, what Maslow calls self-actualised, that is creative, energised, centred, focused and productive.

Maslow's hierarchy offers a clue as to why we think mainly about negative emotions, such as anxiety and fear, when considering children's behaviour. Our most basic instincts are based on the evolutionary needs of fight or flight. Anxiety makes some people become aggressive, others withdrawn. Children (or adults) focus on physical and emotional needs, rather than the higher, social levels, unless the former are met. We all want love and approval to provide us with the security to meet our emotional needs. To become part of a wider group requires a consistency of physical and emotional care. However, intense emotional experiences may make even secure adults revert to meeting more basic needs. Think how seeing a group of loud youths at night may bring back our primal fears of being attacked; or how people's orderly behaviour changes when others threaten them, queuing for a ticket or at the sales.

Children come to school with a pattern of how to regulate emotional responses etched into them from infancy. All children find it hard to learn to relate to other children. Some find it especially hard because of the responses they have experienced at home or in wider society and by the social context in which they live. Powerful emotions, especially anxiety, overcome the inhibitory and regulatory mechanisms which in all young children are fragile, so that quite small events can upset these. For vulnerable children, this will happen quickly and frequently, so that helping them become more resilient may take a great deal of time and effort and is not always successful.

Is it too late to change such patterns of emotional response and behaviour once children reach school age? Awareness of the importance of children's prior experience on how they act and relate to other people helps teachers to understand why most children find socialisation difficult and some find it incredibly hard. A quote used by Barkley (1995) states, *the children who need love the most will always ask for it in the most unloving ways*. Teachers cannot change children's early experiences or the situation in which they live, but a relationship with a trusted and consistent adult and a safe environment can help children to practise appropriate patterns of response and so develop the qualities they need.

As adults, we tend to associate regulating emotional responses with conscious mechanisms, such as telling oneself to calm down when getting muddled cooking a meal or mending a car, or breathing deeply. These usually help to reduce one's anxiety and so lead to more purposeful behaviour, but they are only partially effective or may not work in the face of intense emotion. Many children who crave love and approval lack the background of appropriate relationships and reinforcement to enable them to act so that they receive it. Getting them to try harder is not enough. Nurturing, secure relationships are a prerequisite for developing the qualities to learn to interact appropriately.

Points for consideration and discussion

What qualities do you associate with emotional maturity?

What are the characteristics of a child who is socially developed?

How much should a teacher make allowances for a child who finds social relationships difficult?

How is emotional intelligence linked to social development? What are its limitations?

Emotional Intelligence combines the intrapersonal and interpersonal qualities high-lighted in Chapter 3, with awareness of one's own and other people's emotional responses linking emotional and social development. It emphasises those aspects of learning not covered by the academic curriculum.

The psychologist Daniel Goleman (1996) wrote an accessible book which made emotional intelligence (EI), or emotional literacy, popular. This lies behind many programmes to improve children's behaviour and may be seen as a reaction to the growing emphasis on 'academic' learning. It draws on Gardner's (1993) idea of 'multiple intelligences', which challenges the idea that intelligence is fixed and related only to what can easily be tested. Weare (2004, p2) characterises emotional literacy as *the ability to understand ourselves and other people, and in particular to be aware of, under-stand and use information about the emotional states of ourselves and others with competence. It includes the ability to understand, express and manage our own emotions and respond to the emotions of others, in ways that are helpful to ourselves and others.* It has been broadened both by Goleman and others beyond its original insight, leading to somewhat simplistic views of what teachers should do to build up EI. Claxton (2005) provides an excellent example of how research, well presented, can show the strengths and limitations of a term which gains much of its appeal because it is imprecise. Claxton challenges:

- **the evidence for EI being the basis for success in life;**
- **a limited and at times superficial view of what human emotion involves and the model of the 'good life' that EI takes for granted; and**
- **the view that 'feeling good' or high self-esteem always leads to better learning.**

The next few paragraphs summarise some strengths and weaknesses of EI by explor-ing some claims about its benefits.

EI rightly reminds us that children learning to recognise, to name and to trust their emotional responses tends to make it easier to think about how to regulate or deal with them. For example, it is ridiculous (though I have done it for years!) to pretend not to be angry or delighted when one is. Awareness of one's own emotional responses normally makes it easier to behave appropriately, which is likely to depend on the social and cultural context. For instance, when angry, this may involve smiling sweetly, announcing calmly that one is angry or banging one's fist on the table and shouting; or, when elated, phoning one's parents, going out for a celebra-tory party or privately punching the air.

However, too uncritical an acceptance of certain approaches to EI leads some teachers to think that they should build children's self-esteem by never saying anything negative. While disaffection and low attainment is often the result of low self-esteem, teachers should not just immerse children in a constant stream of uncritical praise. Claxton (2005, p17) cites Dweck's research that self-esteem is much more potent when it is *won through striving whole-heartedly for worthwhile ends rather than derived from praise*, especially praise only loosely related to actual achievement. This type of authentic self-esteem, based on high expectations, provides the basis for intrinsic motivation. For instance, seven-year-old Jack, whose mild autism had led other teachers to praise him effusively whatever he did, only started to write fluently when I, naively but successfully, challenged him to write more than one sentence.

While children who relate to others in an aggressive or withdrawn way cannot alter how they behave simply through will power, they do need to avoid a sense of helplessness and to have a belief that they can change.

Case study

He told me to ...

Sohail came to our school with many difficulties associated with a lack of organisation. He was always getting into trouble – usually of a fairly minor kind – with his typical excuse being that 'he told me to'. Discussions seemed to make little impact though he would recognise that he needed to take his own decisions. On two occasions, I took him outside and asked him if he would lie in the road if I told him to. He said he wouldn't because it would be stupid, but he never connected that with not acting inappropriately when other children told him to. He never seemed to gain a sense of agency – that he needed to take the decisions for himself if his behaviour was going to change.

EI involves the ability to empathise, that is to see the world, as far as possible, from someone else's perspective, for instance by recognising how someone else is feeling. Reciprocal and consistent relationships help children to develop an awareness of other people's views and so to move away from too great an emphasis on themselves. Fairbairn, cited by Storr (1988, p150), sees the final stage of emotional development as *mature dependence*. Empathy provides both a vaccine against, and an antidote to, egocentricity. It requires imagination about how it is to be other than oneself. As with many aspects of SMSC, the activity as such is less important than how it is experienced. Remember that often we need to 'fake it till we make it', that we do not really learn qualities such as empathy until we have experienced what they feel like 'from within'. Such qualities are learnt largely by practice, even when they are only partially developed, rather as one learns to swim by swimming.

Claxton (2005, p30) highlights the greatest danger related to EI as believing that talking fluently about emotion will guarantee what really matters – being emotionally sensitive and adept. I recently saw an articulate nine year old – who had just returned from a demonstration to teachers of how circle time could enhance EI – kicking, really hard, a child who had annoyed her. When challenged, she knew exactly what she 'should' do, but did something quite different. EI involves learning how to act and interact, not just to repeat what one should do like a parrot.

Points for consideration and discussion

What makes it difficult for children to get on with other children?

How much should children's backgrounds affect teachers' expectations?

How important an influence is the peer group?

Why do all children find social development challenging?

Patterns of response and behaviour are established before children start school. For most, these provide a secure foundation, although they still need constant reassurance and guidance. Most children grow up reasonably sociable and well-adjusted – a success we should celebrate – but social development does not always come easily.

In relation to moral development, I suggested that the main difficulty for children was that different influences leave them confused about how to act. The three main ones discussed there – the family, peer group and wider society, especially the media – all affect social development and the complexities of school life must be added.

Any child arriving at school encounters new adults and children to relate to, with the accompanying expectations and uncertainties about whether, and how, to meet them in a range of unfamiliar contexts. This involves (usually with much less structure and support than previously):

- **recognising that one's own wishes are likely to conflict with those of others;**
- **working out where expectations are different from those of one's family or culture.**

Almost all young children find it challenging to move into a bigger setting without the level of adult security to which they are accustomed. For example, some five year olds need a lot of guidance on choosing activities or how to make friends, especially outside the classroom. Making friends is much harder than adults recognise, not least because this involves risk and compromise. I recall one seven year old with a complex family background, saying wistfully that his only friend was the climbing frame. Those who have little experience of secure relationships find it hard to know who to trust and how to go about it. As children reach the age of seven or eight, most become less dependent on one or two specific relationships and more able to cope with a range of adults and approaches.

Nursery or playgroup helps children to understand about interacting in a group. Examples include sharing toys, taking turns, eating together, helping someone in difficulty, all the fabric of social relations. Many children, especially when they first start school, may have had little experience of such interactions and require structure and support to get used to this. This is even more confusing when home and school have different expectations. Different cultural traditions may present uncertainties, such as when a Muslim child is expected to undress for PE with other children, or whether children are expected to make eye contact with adults speaking to them. Although children usually pick up the expected conventions of behaviour remarkably quickly, sensitivity is often required.

More difficult is when the child is told to act in one way by the school and another from home. I have cited the example of children told by parents to hit back, but others include who to play with, what sort of games to play and how to make friends. While these may seem obvious, many children, especially the young and the vulnerable, require quite explicit discussion with the group, the individual child and his or her parents. Some parents have strong views on this, which may be at odds with the school's, and your, approach. Convincing them, or at least trying to, may require a good deal of time and energy, for which it is likely to be wise to involve more experienced colleagues.

As well as formal expectations, informal ones about how children should interact abound, many established by the peer group. Remember as a teacher that you will never know some of these. I recall telling a parent whose son did not know which toilet to use the formal policy, that all the toilet cubicles could be used by both boys and girls. However, the children had a strong but unwritten code of who used which toilet. Similar 'rules' apply to the playground, going to lunch, who can play which game and many other social conventions which children need to negotiate and understand. How the child responds to other children is likely to affect how she or he is accepted, or not, within the group. Those who 'fit in' tend to receive the positive affirmation which helps them to fit in even more. Those left out may easily adopt a self-perpetuating pattern of responses making it even harder to fit into the group.

This section highlights the complexity of what children are expected to understand, not just formal expectations but more informal ones among the children. A school policy, for instance on bullying, may conflict with other messages the child receives at home or from other children. So, social development, while apparently quite obvious, requires a sophisticated understanding of confusing expectations. Most children, supported by their teacher, manage these fine, but all may sometimes feel vulnerable, especially as a result of changing school or class, or personal upset, such as the breakdown of a friendship or parental relationships. So, all children are likely at some time to need additional support, but some, considered in the next section, may require this more often or in specific ways.

Points for consideration and discussion

How much should the child's prior experience affect one's expectations?

Do boys and girls have different needs in terms of social development?

What are the different challenges for children from affluent or deprived backgrounds?

Why is moral and social development so hard for some children?

Because difficulties with moral and social development often go hand in hand, I consider these two together. However, we need to recognise two dangers. The first is always to think that the problem lies with the child or the family. The previous section shows that social expectations are far from obvious. How the school, or the teacher, responds to a child's uncertainty provides valuable support, sometimes with clear, non-negotiable expectations, sometimes with responses to be tailored to individual need. The second danger is that of stereotyping. In regarding a particular group as vulnerable, one must not fall into the trap of thinking that this refers to each individual, which may lead to lowered expectations and so to lower attainment. So, teachers have to tread a difficult path between recognising the challenges which certain groups face and maintaining high expectations of what individuals can achieve in spite of this. While being sensitive to the child's background and circumstances, it is inappropriate to make definite assumptions on the basis of these.

The discussion of attachment and Maslow's hierarchy offers clues as to why many children find social relationships so difficult. Some have internalised how to regulate their emotional responses consistently. Others have gained the confidence about their own identity necessary to build trusting relationships without constant adult support. The challenge of a bigger and unfamiliar environment is especially difficult for those who are vulnerable because of a pattern of insecure or inconsistent relationships and responses. This is most likely with children from very disrupted or difficult backgrounds such as those who are 'looked after' (by the local authority in place of their parents), refugees displaced from their home background and those who have suffered violence or neglect.

Boys find social development especially hard. The evidence for this is both anecdotal and statistical, such as the numbers of those excluded. Fighting and anti-social behaviour seem to be dominated by boys. The reasons are very complicated but because gender identity is, at least in large part, socially constructed, both girls and boys experience strong pressure to conform to the gendered expectations of the family, the peer group and society. Put crudely, boys tend to be encouraged not to express their emotions, to be wary of intimacy and either to interact through emotionally 'safe' activities, such as sport, or to be less dependent on relationships; while girls interact more by developing close relationships. Timimi (2005) presents a challenging analysis of how attention deficit and hyperactivity disorder (ADHD) is a diagnosis often used to 'explain' boys' poor behaviour, resulting in their being medicated. He suggests that the expectations of the family, school and society take too little account of boys' needs, especially for play. Trying to fit children into a mould may help forge an inappropriate identity. A similar process can be seen in how some girls' identity is based on fashion or sexualised behaviour at a young age. Adults tend to reinforce gendered behaviour, for instance by paying more attention to boys who demand adult attention. Although boys' social development occupies a disproportionate amount of teachers' time, do not ignore the needs of girls and of those boys who make fewer direct demands. For a good discussion of how young children's gendered identities are constructed and possible strategies to adopt, see Lloyd and Duveen (1992).

How some children respond is explained, at least partially, by how hard their life is – maybe because of what happens at school, for example, bullying or feeling a failure, or perhaps because of violence or abuse, rejection or lack of adult attention at home. One example seared into my memory is of a ten year old into whose lunchbox

I happened to look one Monday lunchtime. Seeing that it contained only crusts, I asked why. Reluctantly, he disclosed that these were the remains of Friday's lunch and that he had not been home over the weekend but had fended for himself. While this is exceptional, remember that school provides a haven of security for many children, particularly, but by no means exclusively, in deprived urban areas. While many challenges result from poverty, children from affluent families may also find social development difficult. Many find it very hard to consider any needs except their own, possibly because they have had insufficient experience of adult attention, secure boundaries or building up their resilience.

Where does social development take place?

At the start of this chapter, I highlighted Ofsted's emphasis that social development involved children learning to:

- **take responsibility;**
- **show initiative;**
- **work successfully as a member of a team;**
- **show respect for people, living things, property and the environment; and**
- **develop an understanding of living in a community.**

The first three can be summarised as being able to work co-operatively, though the first two are by no means specific to social development. The last two are about how one relates to other people and the world around. None are skills to be taught in discrete, separate ways, but are rather ways of working and attitudes learnt mainly through practice. Children can, and should, be taught rules and strategies, but it is primarily through doing, and through repeated experience of what these feel like, that these become internalised. Children get used to thinking of others, not only of themselves, not through lessons in this but through the experience in group activities of learning how to recognise and draw on each other's strengths, and understanding social relationships in the process of collaborating. It is what children do to, and with, each other that matters, not just being able to 'talk a good game'.

Citizenship and PSHE, circle time and co-operative games offer obvious opportunities for developing teamwork, respect and understanding of each other. However, social development does not happen only in the slots in the timetable when 'we do social development'. As with much of SMSC, it implies a way of working in all aspects of school life, from literacy lessons to the playground, from how children's successes are celebrated to how they are encouraged to ask questions. So, social development is embedded in how class and school environments are created, just as every aspect of school life can be seen in moral terms.

A great genius is usually pictured sitting alone. Most tasks in school are completed individually, with marks taken off if you were found to be using other people's ideas. Competitiveness is often seen as the only spur to people working hard, and doing better, relative both to other people and to their own previous best. Yet learning is a social as well as an individual activity. A school play or concert enable individual achievement, in different ways, and are collective activities where the whole group can achieve more than any one individual could on their own. The same is true of team sport, of singing in a choir or of running an environmental campaign. It is not just that social development enhances learning – though it does – but that learning is rooted in a social and cultural context where learners depend on others rather than ploughing an individual furrow.

This and the previous chapter have highlighted the link between moral and social development. In the next, we consider how actions and interactions are linked to cultural development. Cultural identity affects children's view of themselves and culture and background affects both how people act and how these actions are understood. As Timimi writes (2005, p85), *culture functions to provide a set of values, beliefs and practices to guide a group of people in how to deal with the difficult business of social relationships.*

Recommended reading

Claxton, G (2005) *An Intelligent Look at Emotional Intelligence*. London: Association of Teachers and Lecturers. A short and thoughtful pamphlet, which summarises what teachers should take note of, and be wary of, in thinking about emotional intelligence.

Gerhardt, S (2004) *Why Love Matters: how affection shapes a baby's brain*. Hove: Routledge. An accessible summary of the lessons from brain research about emotional development, with the first two chapters especially useful.

Goleman, D (1996) *Emotional intelligence: why it can matter more than IQ*. London: Bloomsbury. A popular book by a psychologist giving a good background to the importance of emotional and social development.

Lloyd, B and Duveen, G (1992) *Gender Identities and Education*. Hemel Hempstead: Harvester Wheatsheaf. Based on research on gender and identity in Reception with a good discussion of what teachers can and can't do to influence this.

Weare, K (2004) *Developing the Emotionally Literate School*. London: Paul Chapman Publishing. A fairly simple discussion of emotional literacy and what some schools have done to encourage this.

Other references

Barkley, R A (1995) cited on www.russellbarkley.org

Bowlby, J (1965) *Child care and the growth of love*. London: Penguin

Evans, D (2001) *Emotion: A Very Short Introduction*. Oxford: Oxford University Press

Maslow, A (1998) *Toward A Psychology of Being*. New York: Wiley

Ofsted (1999) *Handbook for Inspecting Primary and Nursery Schools*.

Ofsted (2003) *Handbook for Inspecting Primary and Nursery Schools*.

Storr, A (1988) *The School of Genius*. London: Andre Deutsch

Timimi, S (2005) *Naughty Boys*. Basingstoke: Palgrave Macmillan

5 WHAT DOES CULTURAL DEVELOPMENT INVOLVE?

By the end of this chapter you should:

- know about the complexity of how the word 'culture' is used;
- have thought about the different challenges in enhancing cultural awareness depending on children's backgrounds;
- understand more about the link between culture and creativity;
- recognise that all learning takes place within a cultural context;
- have started to consider where opportunities for cultural development occur.

This will help you to meet Standards:
➔ S 1.1, 1.3, 2.4, 3.3.6, 3.3.14

How is the word 'culture' used?

'Cultural' is elusive because we all frequently, often unwittingly, slip between at least three different usages. The first, culture as identity, or belonging, comes from the tending of natural growth, as in agriculture or horticulture, and one's roots. This involves children understanding the groups to which they belong, and similarities and differences of those in other groups, and their associated beliefs and practices. So, Ofsted (1995, p82) states that judgments on cultural development should be based on the extent to which the school *teaches pupils to appreciate their own cultural traditions and the diversity and richness of other cultures.*

A second meaning, based on culture as 'the best that has been thought and said', contrasts 'high culture' (such as opera, classical music or literature) with 'low culture' (such as TV soap operas, pop music or Mills and Boon), designed more for entertainment. This view sees the stories of CS Lewis as 'better' than those of Enid Blyton, ballet and opera preferable to disco-dancing and pop music and the plays of Alan Ayckbourn superior to *EastEnders*. Cultural development here involves introducing children to a broadening and enriching range of experience. Thirdly, culture denotes the environment in which we live, understand and interpret our experiences – as in 'classroom culture' or 'Western culture'. Since those within a culture tend to assume their own beliefs or understandings to be normal, cultural development involves helping children recognise that people have different ways of making sense of what they experience. Culture is organic and dynamic, so that it is constantly being transformed. Cultural development involves children both understanding and learning to transform the world they inhabit. In Ofsted's (2004, p23) words, [cultural development] *is about understanding that cultures are always changing and coping with change.*

All our Futures (NACCCE, 1999, p48) describes the four central roles for education in cultural development as:

- to enable young people to recognise, explore and understand their own cultural assumptions and values;
- to enable young people to embrace and understand cultural diversity by bringing them into contact with attitudes, values and traditions of other cultures;
- to encourage an historical perspective by relating contemporary values to the processes and events that have shaped them;
- to enable young people to understand the evolutionary nature of culture and the processes and potential for change.

While the language may be more appropriate to older children, this indicates that cultural development underlies every subject and is not some marginal extra, but deals, as spiritual development does, with what is most important to us. In Eagleton's (2000, p131) words,

> culture is not only what we live by. It is, also, in great measure, what we live for. Affection, relationship, memory, kinship, place, community, emotional fulfilment, intellectual enjoyment, a sense of ultimate meaning.

Let us think about the cultural influences on ourselves, something of which we are often not very aware. So think, on your own or with others, about which groups you belong to and what makes you a member of each, whether through conscious choice or otherwise. All go to make up who you are.

Points for consideration and discussion

Which of the groups you belong to can you leave? Which are fixed?

Which of these have been most influential in your own development?

How does this affect your learning?

How is identity related to culture?

Think what groups you belong to:

Those which can be changed easily	Those which are permanent or can be changed only with great difficulty

Among the permanent groups may be your family, your blood group or whether you are the carrier of a disease. Others are influenced by early experience, such as one's first language. Modern science has made it possible to change central aspects of our identity, such as gender or the ability to have a child. Those we choose, and so can change, such as the football team you support or the style of your hair, may seem relatively unimportant. Yet most of us find that, in practice, these are rarely, if ever, trivial. TV and fashion, sport and music affect how we relate to each other and how we feel part of a group. We may choose to emphasise, or play down, our Welshness, our political affiliation or our religious faith. Cultural development involves understanding where and how we do – and do not – belong. Think of when you have misunderstood what you are supposed to wear in a particular context – not just finding out too late that it wasn't a fancy-dress party – or have missed a film everyone else is talking about.

In which groups do you really feel 'at home' and why? This may be a club or society, a faith group, a pub, a local community. Now think of groups or contexts where you do not, maybe because you speak differently or your skin colour or gender makes you stand out. The sort of people we are is intimately tied in with the groups to which we do, or do not, belong. Culture both bonds those who do fit in and excludes those who do not. This is in some respects, but only some, a matter of choice.

Belonging provides a framework for security, based on shared expectations. This may be evident in visible symbols of identity, from a brand of clothes or a make of car to markers of religious affiliation or a gay pride badge. Whether these make us feel uncomfortable or proud of what they symbolise depends both on the context and the strength of our feeling of group membership. Markers of identity also work much more subtly. When going into an unfamiliar environment, we have to work out what is expected to know whether we belong or not. A sign of friendliness in one cultural setting may be seen as hostile in another, a mark of respect in one understood as insolence elsewhere. How we express appreciation depends on where we come from and where we are, with the wild banging of feet or cheering appropriate in a club or a children's party, but usually out of place at a wedding or a university graduation.

We all have had the experience of feeling an outsider. If only temporary, this can be amusing. I remember asking, in rural Pakistan, when a bus would leave and, with a look approaching incomprehension, being told, 'When it is full, of course'. But those of you from minority ethnic backgrounds, who are women, or who have a physical disability, will, I am sure, have experienced dislocation more frequently in particular places or sub-cultures. Without someone or something familiar it is difficult to feel comfortable or that we belong. A more permanent feeling of being excluded is frightening and debilitating – worth remembering as you consider young children's cultural development.

What is cultural capital?

All children bring a wealth of experience and expectations accumulated both from their cultural inheritance and since birth, often described as 'cultural capital'. This is like money, where currency acceptable in one country is not in another. In this context, children cannot use it to gain access to what school has to offer. Another analogy is with language. A fluent Spanish speaker can ask for what she wants in a shop in Spain. Someone with only GCSE level Spanish may get what she requires with some difficulty. Very limited Spanish results in an expenditure of a great deal of time, effort and patience. Although all children bring a wealth of experience, those who understand the social and cultural expectations of school have a big advantage. So, the environment and expectations you create help all children to make use of the experience they bring, especially those for whom school is a threatening or unfamiliar place. Children should not be expected to devalue their home and cultural background when they come to school.

Why is cultural development so important?

All children bring to school a range of cultural experiences which has helped to shape who they are. Culture both reflects and structures how we understand, and make sense of, experience, and ourselves. Children create their understanding of the world within a series of cultural frameworks: family, class, school and wider society. For the young child, the most important is the micro-culture of the family, gradually moving towards belonging to the wider community, the class, the school, a town or area, the nation and global citizenship.

As with moral and social development, the influences on cultural development can be seen as:

- **internal to the child, such as low levels of self-esteem or self-belief;**
- **external to the child, such as bullying and racism or a lack of understanding of, or hostility to, cultural traditions, either outside, or sadly within, school.**

However, these are intertwined, because how children make sense of experience depends on both on their cultural background and the context. Experience is understood through the filter of identity. The same experience is experienced differently according to our belief about ourselves. Take the example of walking along a dark street at night. Your reaction is likely to depend both on your age, gender and ethnicity and on your understanding of the experience – as frightening or an adventure, for instance – and your emotional responses, such as fear or excitement.

Cultural, like moral, development depends on both habituation and conscious choice. Much of this occurs where children are incorporated unconsciously – 'this is how we do things here' – into particular ways of relating and responding. For example, racism or bullying occurs much less within a culture, especially in the peer group, where such behaviour is unacceptable. But it also involves helping children to acquire the tools to reflect consciously and critically on what is familiar and what is different, to understand both themselves and other people.

Think of a six year old working out what is appropriate on a school playground. There will be all sorts of clues, some public, most more subtle, such as what other children are doing, who one's friends are, whether one is likely to be accepted. However, that environment is not static. The child's responses may alter it, what is sometimes called a recursive loop. For example, inappropriate responses will make it harder for him or her to be accepted; and by showing confidence the child is more likely to be accepted. One paradox of cultural development is that to belong, you need to have belonged. Those who have little experience of belonging in small groups find it hard to belong in larger ones. Those who belong have their self-esteem and sense of well-being enhanced and so find it easier to belong.

Case study

Boys of Caribbean heritage

Although boys of Caribbean heritage enter school with high levels of attainment relative to other groups, this drops off as they move through primary school and into the secondary years, leading to increased levels of disaffection and exclusion and low GCSE results. The reasons for this are complicated and contested. Schools often blame family structures, including absent fathers, and a culture which does not value education. Families may emphasise racism, both within the wider society and in schools, leading to low academic expectations. Whatever the reason, the failure of schools to draw on these children's and families' cultural capital leads to increasing disaffection linked to low self-esteem and aspirations. These feed each other, so that many black adolescent boys identify with a peer group where identity and status is gained by factors other than, and which militate against, academic success. A system is created which leads to a cycle of disaffection, where identity is gained at the expense of, rather than through, academic attainment. A cycle of low self-esteem can easily become self-perpetuating, where low self-esteem leads to low levels of achievement and to disaffection, which in turn undermines self-esteem. Equally, a cycle of high achievement and positive self-esteem tends to become self-generating.

In Chapter 4, I highlighted challenges facing members of vulnerable groups. Prior experience and the context in which they live make life very hard for the many children who lead chaotic lives with too little adult attention and structure. While teachers cannot change deep-rooted attitudes and beliefs immediately, they can provide protection or support against external pressures for those who are vulnerable – which includes most children at some time. Recognising children's background and family, language and religion can help them to draw on the resources and strengths they bring, which may otherwise be devalued or unacknowledged. For example, many emerging bilinguals bring a knowledge of language often overlooked by schools, and many asylum seekers and refugees have developed enormous resilience and positive attitudes by dealing with difficult situations.

So try to see what is unfamiliar but forms part of the individual child's identity in positive terms. But be careful to avoid stereotyping, which may lower your expectations and children's aspirations. For example, many children from minority ethnic backgrounds benefit from the support of a wide family network, where others are much less secure, especially where the family has experienced dislocation or racism.

While many middle-class parents find it easier to support their children when the going gets tough, whether because of wealth, their own educational success or access to the teacher, some do not find enough time to provide the attention and care necessary to develop qualities such as empathy or resilience.

Describing the large, successful inner-city school he ran in Birmingham, Winkley (2002, pp316–17) wrote:

> Hunters succeed best by far in the middle-class world where hunting can in some measure be an add-on, a game founded on a strong sense of culture … For poorer and less stable people, the hunting psychology is a disaster unless the individual has a powerful and sustained self-belief. Which is why strong cultural and family traditions and communal pride are so important … It may be, then, that what matters most in schools in (deprived) areas like this is that we should be producing such farmers – children with practised skills and pride in their culture, in their background, and most of all in themselves.

His school managed to combine this cultural pride with high aspirations and achievements in all areas of learning, from outstanding music based on a range of cultural traditions, to children, when appropriate, learning mathematics and other subjects at levels not normally introduced until secondary school.

Introducing children to the stories, festivals and customs of different cultures and faiths provides the chance for the whole class to experience and understand the diversity of an increasingly global society. For children to learn about and respect their own and other cultures cannot be separated from values and beliefs, especially in Key Stage 2. Education for cultural diversity must therefore not concentrate only on what is out of the ordinary, but must help children to be respectful of what is unfamiliar, to recognise commonality as well as difference, and to learn about, and be critical of, their own and other people's culture. For example, learning about India should involve knowing about its wealth as well as its poverty, and may entail judgments about the caste system as well as the Taj Mahal. Similarly, learning about French culture should include the fact that they eat fast food as well as baguettes and snails, and have a history of war and empire, as well as wonderful films and literature.

Children need both to compare and contrast other cultures with their own – and this involves knowing about and exercising critical judgment about what is familiar as well as what is strange. This can be very tricky where the values of a particular culture may clash with your own – for example, in my case, relating to some cultures' attitudes towards women or absolute certainty on moral questions.

Case study

Single-sex or mixed swimming?

One dilemma I faced as the head of a first school related to swimming. An increasing number of Muslim children, mostly girls, were not taking part.

An investigation showed that many Muslim parents were unhappy about mixed-sex groups. The Muslim families were a minority, though a substantial one, and made fewer requests than white middle-class parents. I thought that single-sex swimming would show the willingness of the school community to respond to this strongly felt belief. After discussion with governors, this was introduced. A huge debate ensued, with many non-Muslim parents passionately and volubly opposed. In the end, it was agreed that the norm should be single-sex, with those who wanted mixed swimming able to opt for that. One middle-class parent, initially opposed, but ultimately more sympathetic, said to me, 'We all love the school's multicultural nature, but this is the first time we have ever been asked to give up anything we care strongly about.'

Points for consideration and discussion

Was there an issue at all? Should this just have been ignored and the Muslim parents told that their children had to join in?

How does one balance the needs of different cultural or religious groups?

To what extent is it the teacher's role to introduce children to a common cultural heritage?

I am not suggesting that, as a teacher, let alone a newly qualified one, you are likely to face such difficult decisions yourself. But I tell the story so that you recognise that questions of culture can be extremely contentious.

Is there a common culture to which children should be introduced?

One's own culture cannot be properly understood without knowing the historical influences which shape it. Unless children know certain Bible stories – David and Goliath, Jonah and the whale and Jesus' life, for example – they miss out on a common cultural inheritance, essential to understanding literature or art, as well as wonderful, archetypal stories. This raises the question of how much children should be introduced to a common culture. Should the Judaeo-Christian moral tradition form the basis of a common approach to moral education? Should those applying for citizenship be tested on their linguistic competence or knowledge of British history? Should all children have to study certain authors from the canon of English literature? Such questions of national identity have emerged in the last 30 years or so, as society has become ethnically and culturally more diverse, more geographically mobile and affected by a wider range of influences.

Points for consideration and discussion

How much is there a common culture, both as a society and in your own area?

Which features of our culture do you think all children should know about?

How can one most successfully help children understand about diversity?

This is a difficult area. An appeal to common culture can easily become a code for dislike of unfamiliar people or practices, and at times for racism. This may range from disapproving of rap music and only thinking of classical music as worthwhile, to suspicion of children learning about other faiths or visiting different places of worship, to moving children to another school because too many children come from backgrounds other than white, English-speaking ones.

In some respects, culturally and ethnically diverse schools are in a privileged position. They can draw on diverse resources – people, buildings and artefacts – in their local community easily. In rural schools or those in homogeneous areas, extending the range of children's cultural awareness is even more important, but potentially more difficult, because children may have never, or only rarely, seen people from other ethnic backgrounds and faiths. Colleagues or parents may see this as unimportant or as a distraction from raising standards of attainment. Those in a school with a Christian foundation may be suspicious of introducing children to other faiths. So be sensitive to the culture of the school and community you teach in – but remember that you can also help to shape it.

To what extent does cultural development involve introducing children to 'high' culture?

Schools operate within a social and political context. We have considered the influences and values of the family and the peer group. However, many of the strongest cultural influences come from advertising, television, the Internet and video games. Whatever the potential to benefit children's learning by extending their intellectual and cultural knowledge and horizons, these influences present considerable challenges, partly because of how long children are exposed to them, partly because of the sophisticated way in which messages are presented. For example, their visual images engage children's interests in ways that most teachers struggle to match. Their immediacy runs counter to thoughtful, reflective responses.

Much of the media is based on cultures of sport, of fashion, of celebrity, offering instant and undemanding enjoyment. The electronic media rarely require children to be critical of what they see or, when they are physically and mentally active, as in a video game, offer little control of, or the opportunity to question, the material presented. One of my particular concerns is how violence is commonplace, whether in zapping aliens or in films which show pain and death as a matter of course.

Children live in a society where happiness is presented as being dependent on possession and consumption, with the pursuit of happiness largely an individual quest. This is, moreover, based on an increasingly standardised view – though the media are shrewd enough to pay lip service to cultural diversity. So children – indeed all of us – are encouraged to be consumers and to seek immediate gratification through possession and appearance. The emphasis is on having rather than on being, on ownership rather than experience. Such messages are often in conflict with those that SMSC raises, involving an exploration of who one is and where one fits in, based on less transient values.

Points for consideration and discussion

How would you criticise this analysis of society's values?

Are the messages from the media really just harmless enjoyment?

How much should you introduce young children to other influences?

Of course, children need to enjoy themselves; and you may think that much of what they see on TV or the games they play is just harmless entertainment. While research can never be conclusive, the evidence about how learning bypasses consciousness should make us wary of scenes that portray casual use of violence, and with some people being seen as worthwhile and others as objects of derision or scorn.

While you may see me as a killjoy or a grumpy old man, or probably both, part of education's role is to introduce young children to elements of culture which do not offer immediate and easily accessible gratification. This is both to balance the entertainment that occupies a large part of most children's lives and to sow the seeds for children to learn to appreciate, and engage with, a wider range of cultural activities. Cultural development involves introducing children to experiences which, when worked at, extend our understanding and enjoyment and enrich us in ways that are hard to fathom, let alone measure.

Introducing children to 'high' culture, designed to 'improve' them, risks imposing a particular view of what is worthwhile on children – most of whom are likely to be keener on more accessible entertainment. One may be accused of imposing middle-class values and so devaluing those of the child's home and some activities from which children derive tremendous pleasure. But, as with all of SMSC, adults have to make judgments about what is authentic and worthwhile. Teachers, in practice, do that all the time. A second danger is children may be put off classical music or high quality literature if it is presented inappropriately. Successful provision may involve outsiders such as Theatre in Education or Artists in Residence introducing children to a Shakespeare play or new ways of working with three-dimensional materials. It may draw on existing strengths and interests, as when I introduced a group of Year 6 children to jazz and, without realising it, prompted two girls to create a dance using their wonderful disco-dancing skills. Or it may involve helping children to listen to different types of music, to enjoy poetry, or to understand, compare and evaluate the work of graphic artists.

Points for consideration and discussion

How is cultural development linked to creativity?

How can teachers encourage children to be more creative?

What are the practical problems of encouraging children to be more creative?

How is culture linked to creativity?

'Creativity' is yet another word whose exact meaning is hard to pin down. While creativity and culture are often linked, it is not obvious quite why. In this section, I explore what creativity entails and suggest that it is a way of learning, to be embedded across the whole curriculum.

All Our Futures (NACCCE, p29) defines creativity as:

> *imaginative activity fashioned so as to produce outcomes that are both original and of value.*

This has three important implications. First, it links imagination to originality, of which *All Our Futures* (NACCCE, p30) distinguishes three types: **historic**, **relative**, and **individual**. Historic originality is confined to a few geniuses. Relative originality occurs when a child takes an approach or arrives at an outcome which is original compared to that of other children. Individual originality relates to the child's previous work, so that a dance where a child tries out a series of movements or discovers a mathematical pattern new to him or herself is said to be original. Relative and individual originality roughly correspond with what Craft (Craft et al., pp 45-62) calls 'little c creativity', with big C creativity reserved for historic originality. So young children can be creative without having to make a discovery that is original — except to themselves.

Secondly, the mention of 'outcomes of value' implies producing something worthwhile. Unfortunately, much of what passes for creative activity, such as following detailed instructions to the letter or designing but not making artefacts, is passive and does not result in any worthwhile end-product — which might be a spoken or written sentence, a painting or a series of physical movements. Creative activity implies divergence from established norms and convergence towards an original outcome. Bringing the creative process to an end-product often stops creativity being self-indulgent and helps to focus the mind. However, this definition seems to omit something essential — that the outcome is not predetermined at the start, but adapted in the course of the activity.

Thirdly, the emphasis on activity and the word 'fashioned' implies creativity does not just happen, but has to be worked at. Among the features of 'little c creativity' is the willingness to challenge preconceptions and received wisdom. Creativity is found in, rather than put into, children. But it develops within a cultural tradition, using other people's understandings and techniques. Worthwhile creative activity does not therefore just mean letting children loose with some materials and seeing what happens. It involves children experimenting and organising their experiences in a meaningful way, drawing on, but not being over-constrained by, previous approaches or external dictat. The older the child, the more the teacher may have to encourage such divergence.

All Our Futures (NACCCE, p 89) distinguishes between teaching for creativity and teaching creatively. It is possible to teach creatively without encouraging creativity, and even good creative teaching may leave some children without enough structure within which to exercise their own creative abilities. So think more about teaching for creativity and helping children to be creative learners. This involves them being prepared to:

- **try out new experiences and ways of working;**
- **make unusual connections or adopt different approaches;**
- **use imagination;**
- **be playful;**
- **live with uncertainty.**

All are qualities which young children exhibit and which adults tend both to lose in ourselves and inhibit in children. Teaching for creativity implies empowering, encouraging and enabling children through a range of open-ended activities.

At one level, culture and creativity are linked because the arts are central to the development of individuals and of society. However, the link runs much deeper. Bruner, a psychologist, presents learning as a creative process, whereby a child continually makes sense of experience by formulating new understandings. Learning involves a process of construction, rather than delivery. This does not occur in a vacuum, but culture provides the structure within which, whether we like it or not, learning occurs. So, *culture provides the tools for organising and understanding our worlds in communicable ways* (1996, p3). Culture is not static, since it both shapes us and we re-shape it. Because we create who we become and can do this only within culture, culture provides the framework which shapes our understanding and expectations of ourselves as individuals, as part of larger groups. While Bruner stresses the importance of agency in learning, he emphasises collaboration to show that learning is not simply an individual quest but a social process within a cultural framework.

What are the esssential features of cultural development?

Cultural development helps children to experience and understand: where they belong, and the similarities and differences between themselves and other people; the influences that shape their own and other cultures; how to understand themselves and make sense of experience; how they can actively create and alter how they understand the world. This is achieved through a process of habituation, reflection and change, so reaching beyond the boundaries of their prior experience and learning to be critical of, and see beyond, the framework of beliefs, values and practices in which they grow up.

In previous chapters I have argued that all that happens in school has moral and social implications. Similarly, cultural development extends beyond providing a wide range of opportunities to visit museums and theatres or children learning about different cultures, important as these are. It involves children learning to belong and understand where they fit in.

Recommended reading

Bruner, J (1996) *The Culture of Education*. Cambridge, MA: Harvard University Press. A very thoughtful book on how education is necessarily linked to culture and how culture shapes a child's understanding of the world.

Craft, A, Jeffrey, B and Leibling, M (eds) (2001) *Creativity in Education*. London: Continuum. A useful collection of articles of which several in the first section, up to page 91, address what is discussed in this chapter.

NACCCE (National Advisory Committee on Creative and Cultural Education) (1999) *All Our Futures: Creativity, Culture and Education*. London: DfEE. A report commissioned by Government, which deals with complicated questions very readably and thoughtfully.

Wilson, A (ed.) (2005) *Creativity in Primary Education*. Exeter: Learning Matters. Especially Chapters 1 and 2, which explain the context and different aspects of creativity.

Other references

Eagleton, T (2000) *The Idea of Culture*. Oxford: Blackwell

Ofsted (1995) *Guidance on the Inspection of Nursery and Primary Schools*.

Ofsted (2004) *Promoting and evaluating pupils' spiritual, moral, social and cultural development*. www.ofsted.gov.uk/publications HMI 2125

Winkley, D (2002) *Handsworth Revolution: The Odyssey of a School*. London: de la Mare

6 HOW DOES SPIRITUAL, MORAL, SOCIAL AND CULTURAL DEVELOPMENT FIT IN WITH THE REST OF CHILDREN'S LEARNING?

By the end of this chapter you should:

- *understand more about common themes linking the four elements of SMSC;*
- *have considered the wider implications for the whole range of children's learning;*
- *recognise the importance of children creating a coherent personal narrative;*
- *have started to consider the implications for an appropriate teaching environment.*

This will help you to meet Standards:
➔ *S 1.1, 1.2, 1.3, 2.4, 2.7, 3.2.4, 3.3.1, 3.3.9, 3.3.14*

I have argued that personal development, and SMSC, deals with essential questions about how children learn and should be educated. You are probably wondering how this fits in, or conflicts, with the emphasis on literacy, numeracy and behaviour management (what is often called the 'standards agenda') in the Standards for Achieving QTS, the rest of your course and the schools where you teach. This chapter draws together themes about how young children learn, exploring how some enrich and some challenge the standards agenda and discussing some possible objections. In making provision for SMSC, you have to take account of children's other needs and other pressures and constraints. A difficult challenge, but the rest of this book is designed to help you consider how.

The previous four chapters have explored each element of SMSC as a facet or dimension of personal development, a journey of self discovery. This involves questions such as:

Spiritual	Moral
Who am I? Where do I fit in? Why am I here?	How should I act? What sort of person do I want to become?
Social	**Cultural**
How should I interact with other people?	Where do I belong? What is my identity?

Such a view is both exciting and unsettling. It is inevitably personal. I have encouraged you to engage with research findings because their insight, and programmes developed from them, can help make you a better teacher. Most research about learning has been done by psychologists with a background in measurement and cognitive development. Recent insights into how the brain works have led to assertive claims about the mind and how children learn. However, trying to understand the mysterious and complex process of children's learning tends to raise questions rather than provide definitive answers. So, be cautious about any claim that research – or a book like this – offers the answer to all your questions. Reflective teachers balance the immediate task of what to do next with wrestling with basic questions about how children learn and the aims of education. These are too often presupposed and, depressingly, rarely discussed.

Why is emotional development so important?

Let us start by thinking about times when you tried to learn something for the first time. In completing this chart, try to recapture how you felt and what helped you learn better. Add a few of your own. If you haven't yet learnt these, use your imagination!

This shows that: our emotional state affects how we learn, whether as adults or children; being a novice learner is often confusing and difficult; and learning requires appropriate support.

As we have seen, the relationship with the prime-carer influences profoundly how babies relate to, and understand, the world and how the older child manages relationships and responses. Neuroscience suggests the young child's brain remains plastic, but gradually, in Lewis' (2000, pp274–5) words, *thoughts and feelings ... come to form a structure of neurophysiological reflexes*. Lewis goes on to quote Bohm: *Through repetition, emotional intensity and defensiveness, these reflexes have become 'hard-wired' in consciousness, to such an extent that they respond independently of conscious choice.* While this emphasises negative aspects, positive emotional experience and response also helps to reinforce the formation of neural pathways.

As children mature, a wider range of influences comes into play, such as:

- the child's own experience outside school, such as the levels of adult support, chances for discussion or opportunities for extending cultural horizons;
- what happens at school, such as teachers', or other children's, expectations or the curriculum offered;

- the values expressed in society, including the example offered in the media or by other people. As Bruner (1996, p38) states, *school, more than we have realized, competes with myriad forms of anti-school as a provider of agency, identity and self-esteem – no less at a middle-class suburban mall than on the ghetto streets.*

While conscious choice becomes increasingly important, early experience, responses and relationships continue to affect how young children regulate their emotions and behaviour. Uncertainty provokes powerful emotional reactions, especially anxiety, which inhibit our ability to learn. Unless children's emotional needs are met, all learning is impaired. As a teacher, you cannot alter the child's prior experience and have only a limited impact on the wider pressures from society. However, an environment which offers security, nurturing relationships and high but realistic expectations and challenges can help children to regulate their responses appropriately and so develop protective qualities. Nurture is especially important for those unsettled by negative experience when younger or outside school. So, the framework of support that teachers can provide helps children understand, and create an increasingly coherent narrative about, themselves. In the next two sections, we explore what support is needed and what a coherent narrative means.

Points for consideration and discussion

How does a child become the sort of person s/he does?

Whose responsibility is it to determine this?

How do we as adults help young people to develop appropriate values?

What sort of support does young children's personal development require?

Ultimately, whether we like it or not, children choose, consciously or otherwise, the sort of person they become. It is unrealistic for parents, let alone teachers, to try and determine this. As adults our role is to help, support and guide children in actively creating their own identity and character by providing a framework of values. The environment or culture you create helps provide security and structure without which children are left confused by, and unprotected from, a range of other influences. But such a framework is always transitional.

You may think that much of what I have discussed about SMSC relates more to older children. While identity and values are most obviously explored during adolescence, often leading to questioning, or rejecting, what parents or teachers hold dear, I hope that you recognise the importance of early experience. The younger the child, the more important an environment of 'this is how we do things here' is, but it remains so throughout primary school and beyond, so that appropriate action becomes 'second nature', which Young (1994, p116) describes as *history, culture and personal experience disguised as first nature or biology.* But to internalise their own values children need to reflect on their own actions and act appropriately through reason, as well as habit. Ideas such as values and virtues can help children think about, understand, and develop, individual and interpersonal qualities. Expectations from the home, school and elsewhere create aspirations which help, or hinder, this process. How adults model values, in their actions, helps children see what these abstract ideas 'look like' in practice.

At primary school, children can develop qualities and internalise values to meet the challenges of adolescence when such a framework provides less security. Let me make an analogy with boys and singing. Most adolescent boys are too embarrassed to continue singing as their voices break. Their later singing ability is usually enhanced if they can be persuaded to continue trying. However, previous experience of singing provides a foundation they never entirely lose, even if they do give up as adolescents. The risks – in personal development as in music – are that if children are allowed to drift they lack direction and if the framework is too constricting they reject it entirely in adolescence.

'Scaffolding' is a metaphor to describe how a more experienced learner creates a temporary supporting structure to be gradually dismantled as the apprentice learner becomes more confident. Adult interventions can help, or hinder, children to create coherent accounts of their lives through the relationships and social interactions they make. The wrong sort of intervention can easily lead to increased anxiety, or, in the longer term, a loss of self-belief. In Timimi's words (2005, p216) *when adults bring attention to children's failures and the ways they do not measure up to educational and/or behavioural expectations, children then enter into a worldview and self-narrative of incompetence.* This story illustrates the importance of emotional scaffolding from the most unlikely source.

Case study

Skating

As a deputy head, I took a class skating on an end-of-year outing, and was persuaded on to the ice for only the second time ever. I was scared, but learnt a lot about learning. Hardly anyone took my fears seriously. The competent people who said how easy it was were no help at all. Those who laughed at my incompetence were a hindrance. The most valuable support came from David, a child who found life difficult. Mine was one of the few cars he did not shower with gravel when I drove past on the way home. He literally took me by the hand, and led me round. He gave me simple, one-at-a-time instructions. He told me to experiment and skated alongside. He let me make mistakes without bombarding me with advice, encouraging me to skate on my own, returning from time to time to see how I was getting on. And I learnt, as a novice, though I have never acquired a secure identity as a skater.

What does a coherent personal narrative mean?

In Chapter I, I suggested that all approaches to teaching are based on a theory about how children learn. These influence profoundly how teachers work. It is time to make my own theory explicit. This is perhaps best expressed by Pollard (1985, px) who describes symbolic interactionism (not a term I find very useful) as:

founded on the belief that people 'act' on the basis of meanings and understandings which they develop through interaction with others Individuals are thought to develop a concept of 'self' as they interpret the responses of other people to their own actions. Although the sense of self is first developed in childhood, interactionists argue that it is continually refined in later life and that it provides the basis for thought and behaviour.

This indicates why the experiences encountered and the qualities developed influence children's thought and behaviour across the curriculum and throughout their lives. Learning, especially personal development, is a creative and dynamic process based on a concept of self, or identity. Early relationships affect internal qualities which influence how young children understand and respond to the external world. Personal identity is created not delivered.

Points for consideration and discussion

To what extent do you share, or challenge, this view of the self?

What underlying assumptions does this make about children's learning?

Do you believe that your role as a teacher is to explain the world to children?

Vygotsky (1978) is usually associated with intellectual development, emphasising how language helps us to structure reality and develop higher order thinking skills. However, his theory stresses that meaning is embedded in the structures of language and culture and the internalisation of meaning requires interaction, with children constructing knowledge and meaning for themselves. Even experienced learners are always in a state of approximation towards what they are learning, always elaborating an incomplete understanding. All learning involves making sense of experience of which our understanding is only partial. Just as literacy is about making sense of text, of mathematics of patterns, or science of the world, SMSC involves children in integrating fragmentary, often conflicting, experience by constant refinement, or elaboration. Based on a constantly shifting sense of self and identity, they seek to make sense of such experience through an increasingly coherent personal narrative about themselves.

Think how your description of yourself, and your actions, change according to context, as child or parent, as teacher or student, with unfamiliar people or with friends. A great success, or personal tragedy, or the birth of a child, will almost certainly change fundamentally one's narrative about oneself. Just as we have multiple identities and belongings, we have multiple, constantly shifting narratives, which we tell both to ourselves and to other people. Narratives both help to make sense of our experiences and structure how we understand them. The story we tell about ourselves changes, depending on experience, context and how we understand ourselves. The same is true of children as they construct narratives of increasing in complexity. As Macintyre (1999, p216) writes, *deprive children of their stories and you leave them unscripted, anxious stutterers in their actions as in their words.* Children's understanding of themselves will change as they become more certain of where they fit in, learn to control feelings of jealousy or make new friends.

In one sense, making sense of a confusing world is an individual task. However, we have seen the importance of culture in how children understand experiences and themselves. Learning is a social and interactive process, situated within a cultural and historical framework (see Bruner and Haste (1987) for a good account of this). So, children face the paradoxical challenge of making sense of themselves as individuals within something bigger, without becoming too centred on his or her own self, or ego. Hay and Nye (1998, p18) cite Whitehead's view that to think of existence as independent is a mistake. In Archbishop Desmond Tutu's words (Krog, 1999, p165), *a person is human precisely in being enveloped in the community of other human beings, in being caught up in the bundle of life. To be ... is to participate.* Or to quote the poet John Donne, *No man is an Island, entire of itself: every man is a piece of the Continent, a part of the main.*

Part of the power of personal narrative is that it helps make sense of experience while remaining flexible. In Winterson's (1996, p91) words, [stories are] ... *a way of explaining the universe while leaving the universe unexplained, it's a way of keeping it alive, not boxing it into time.* Probably the most fundamental challenge to this view comes from those who bring a definite explanation of the meaning or workings of the world — what is often called a meta-narrative. For example, that meaning comes from God's intervention in the world or that the world can be explained entirely by science. You may hold such a view. I am not arguing whether you are right or wrong, but presenting this inflexibly to children is likely to prevent them constructing and internalising a view of themselves in relation to the world. A narrative which is adopted rather than constructed may be fragile and brittle, so that, especially during adolescence, it is rejected in its entirety when one part is challenged. So, whether you provide a powerful meta-narrative or not, children must be encouraged and enabled to ask questions and learn to accept that no narrative explains everything.

One key question is whether children benefit from articulating their narrative in words. While this may be appropriate for some children, others may do so in a variety of ways, such as play or drawing. Often, children make sense of their experience through their actions. I remember one six year old being unable to talk about a terrible tragedy he had witnessed, but expressing his feelings through play. However, a quiet seven-year-old girl recently surprised me by saying, 'I have one older brother and sister. When I am older I want to study science because I want to become a doctor and you need to be good at science to do that.' I am not advocating that children of primary school age should have their life ahead mapped out for them. But even very young children can be helped to put their past experiences into perspective and think about the future by expressing, in some way, how they make sense of them.

Points for consideration and discussion

What sort of story, or narrative, would you tell about yourself as a learner?

What good learning habits do you have? Which do you need to develop?

Which qualities help to protect children from confusion and giving up to easily?

What qualities in a child contribute to SMSC?

If children are actively to help shape who they become, they have to be able to draw on, and develop, qualities. These may be called habits or dispositions or attitudes, but this raises the contentious question of whether children's actions and responses depend on nature or nurture, on genes or environment. It seems enough, for now, to recognise that patterns of response may be deeply ingrained without necessarily being inherent or transmitted genetically and that people can change.

Most of the qualities of a good learner are not specific to SMSC, but I try to highlight in this section those which contribute most to personal development. Some seem to be acquired only with a struggle, while others come more naturally to children and are often inhibited with maturity. Some may be seen as primarily protective, to help children cope with the challenges of learning, and some more creative and trans-formational, recalling that one distinctive aspect of being human is the ability to be creative in ordinary everyday living.

Claxton and 'learnacy'

Claxton (2002) has coined the term 'learnacy' to signify those habits and dispositions involved in 'learning-to-learn' – becoming better at learning, rather than just learning better. He highlights four, which he calls the 4Rs, which are all interlinked:

- **resilience;**
- **reflectiveness;**
- **reciprocity;**
- **resourcefulness;**

Resilience involves managing distractions, coping with difficulties and persevering. We have seen how young children inhabit a world with confusing messages, which requires them to be persistent and able to overcome difficulties. Among the factors which Herman (2001, p58) cites as helping survivors of trauma are: *an alert, active tempera-ment, unusual sociability and skill in communicating with others, and a strong sense of being able to control their own destiny.* While many children's resilience is low as a result of prior experience or external circumstances, a calm, firm and consistent approach from carers and teachers will provide the protective framework within which resili-ence is most likely to be developed. For example, in Ofsted's (2005, p2) words, *very good whole-school systems to eradicate bullying reduced the risks of pupils developing mental health difficulties.* A balance needs to be struck between too much support, which may make children too dependent, and too little which leaves some vulnerable.

Encouraging and expecting children to be reflective is part of good teaching. This requires children (and us) to be able to reflect, to slow down, to allow our uncon-scious to work, a point further discussed in Claxton (1997). If children are to be encouraged to make sense of the more profound questions about their lives, they need the space to reflect and to answer these for themselves. Remember how busy and cluttered many children's lives are. Kimes Myers (1997, p63), borrowing from Nouwen, describes as *'hospitable'* – *the space in which old and new experiences are accepted, dealt with and transcended.* Some children need this nurturing, hospitable space frequently, because of the pressures they experience, others only at certain times. But we never entirely lose our need for it. As the playwright David Hare says, we all need both haven and challenge.

SMSC requires thoughtfulness, both in responding in a considered way, rather than impulsively, and bearing in mind other people's feelings. Teachers often do not enable reflectiveness for two main reasons: an emphasis on pace and a tendency (which we all share!) to intervene too soon and provide answers. The current approach to literacy and numeracy emphasises pace, for instance in mental arithmetic or spelling. However, SMSC suggests that children do not learn best by being challenged the whole time. Immediate answers to questions about the reasons for global warming or one's own identity are likely to be superficial. Too persistent an emphasis on challenge gives too little time for reflection. Slowing down can help academic learning, but even more so the deeper learning, the sort of deep-seated questions with which SMSC is concerned. Self-discovery needs space as well as pace, particularly the space to dream, to imagine, to pretend. Perhaps the most surprising ability listed by the Mental Health Foundation (cited in Ofsted, 2005, p4) of children who are mentally healthy is that of being able to use and enjoy solitude. Children need the chance to be alone in a life that is often too busy and full of activity.

The attachment so vital in emotional and social development depends on early relationships. Learning is a process where the child is not just a passive recipient but creates new understanding through interaction with others, both adults and children. Appropriate feedback, especially in SMSC, from adults is based on relationships and reciprocity. Much of learning is collaborative and social, with good learners able to work interdependently as well as independently, to test out ideas with other people, and to collaborate. So, social development involves learning to empathise with how other people are feeling, and spiritual development is often associated with compassion, being able to share in someone else's sadness. Relationships both provide support at times of trouble and are integral to knowing who we are and where we fit in.

The last of the 4Rs – resourcefulness – brings us back again to the importance of agency, rather than over-reliance on adults. Personal development seems, necessarily, to require particular qualities and values, some protective, some transformational or creative. As we saw in discussing moral and cultural development, many are widely agreed, though some will vary between cultures. Among those discussed in previous chapters – though you may, rightly, prioritise others or add your own – are the ability to be:

Protective	Transformational
Resilient	Active
Resourceful	Curious
Reciprocal	Creative
Reflective	Playful
Sociable	Imaginative
Interdependent	Critical

Some, such as thoughtfulness, insight and enthusiasm, seem to belong in both columns. In Chapters 7 and 8 we return to how to help develop such qualities.

Points for consideration and discussion

What other qualities would you add to these?

Which good qualities do young children have that adults tend to lose?

What sort of adult intervention encourages, or inhibits, imagination or openness?

How does SMSC challenge common assumptions about learning?

SMSC challenges some commonly held beliefs about learning, arguing (in most cases) not so much that they are wrong, but incomplete. Remember the idea of learning as elaboration, building on previous understanding. In this section, we look at briefly at four misconceptions.

Case study

Emotional difficulties

My first Year 6 class included one boy, Jason, whom I found incredibly difficult. His writing was completely incomprehensible, though it went on for pages, he was very reluctant to take any advice and he would disrupt creative dance lessons by calling out 'Are we doing fairies again?' It was easy to dismiss him as 'not very bright'. Just two incidents, in four terms, made me think otherwise. Once, in front of the whole class, I was trying unsuccessfully to get a tape recorder to work. Despite my best efforts to fix it without blustering I clearly was getting nowhere. With a quiet 'Here give it me,' Jason took it, unscrewed the plug and had it working within a minute or so. Dim? Unintelligent? The second time was when, for a reason I now forget, he drew an elephant, sketching and shading with the deftness of a master draughtsman. Never again. He had learnt that his skills were largely unvalued – until he became an electrician. And his emotional difficulties meant that he had learnt not to take risks.

The first misconception is that intelligence is fixed. Intelligence is strongly associated with ability as measured by tests and recorded on a scale of ability. The underlying assumption is that this measures innate ability and that the abilities which really matter are largely in language and mathematics. Although this has altered, it remains deep within how we see children. Think, for instance, how often we talk about children as 'bright', when really we mean good at reading or mathematics, or how the support for children with special educational needs is nearly always in the same subjects – though this may be entirely appropriate.

Gardner and multiple intelligences

Gardner (1993), a psychologist, originally proposed seven types of intelligence:

- **linguistic;**
- **logical-mathematical;**
- **musical;**
- **bodily-kinaesthetic;**
- **spatial;**
- **interpersonal;**
- **intrapersonal.**

Later he suggested that spiritual should be added. Such a list can be argued over and refined, but such an approach helps teachers think about learners and learning differently. Those interested in 'gifted and talented' often use multiple intelligences to identify aptitudes and abilities in children who do not score highly in conventional IQ tests. Ideas such as Emotional Intelligence help to avoid the trap of thinking about intelligence too narrowly. Gardner's work challenges the view that teaching is mainly about helping children acquiring information and skills. It has led many teachers to rethink what intelligence is and to recognise the importance of offering a broad range of experiences.

The second misconception is that education is primarily about children acquiring skills, especially in literacy and numeracy. Although electronic technology has made the amount and range of information available in a few seconds, even to a young child, larger than could have been imagined twenty, let alone a hundred, years ago, we continue, especially in assessment, to emphasise gathering and memorising chunks of information. Learning involves making links between different sorts of information, knowledge and experience, and exercising critical judgment about what is true and about what is useful. Most seriously, thinking of learning as primarily about skills and information risks overlooking education's role in understanding the most fundamental aspects of human experience. More practically, it tends to lead to a belief that it can be acquired into small chunks, which brings two dangers:

- **reductionism – like believing that a house is only made up of parts such as tiles, planks and cement – when personal development involves integrating these into something bigger than the parts;**
- **short-termism – whereas the journey of self-discovery involves the exploration and internalising of values, beliefs and qualities, all of which are learnt both subtly and over a long period of time.**

The third misconception is that learning is always a linear and cumulative process. In some ways, it obviously is, but Donaldson (1984 and especially 1992) challenges this in relation to intellectual development. She presents learning as involving new modes of understanding as an extension of the child's repertoire, rather than moving from one stage to the next and (so to speak) discarding the previous approach. Our consideration of whether children do develop spiritually challenges whether personal development should be seen in a linear way. One valuable lesson I learnt early on as a teacher was to see the primary years as worthwhile in their own right, not simply as a preparation for secondary school or adult life. The journey of self-discovery seems much more like searching and trying to make sense of our lives, working one's way, hesitantly, towards a destination that is never entirely clear.

Case study

Play!

My doctoral research involved a lot of sitting around watching and listening to four and five year olds. In one unit, there was one very challenging and aggressive boy, often in confrontation with adults. One day, he button-holed me, sat me down, got some construction bricks out and said, loudly, 'Play!' I shuffled a few bricks while he got quite absorbed in constructing a castle, a world safer than that of external reality. Every time he saw me watching or taking notes he reminded me to play. When I put a brick where he didn't want it, he would move it, usually with a sigh or a frown. He was in charge and totally absorbed for some forty-five minutes, ordering the bricks more easily than he could his experiences, while I found it hard to play, as adults tend to.

The fourth misconception is to see learning as always a serious business, with play dismissed as unimportant and not really associated with 'proper' learning. Most parents understand that play is important, an insight backed by a long tradition in the education of young children, from Montessori and Froebel through to the present Foundation Stage Curriculum. This is wrong, not only because the child is in charge and engaged in an activity that is enjoyable and exploratory, but because play enables the child to imagine and to construct a world where different responses can be explored without having to bear the emotional consequences. It is worth pondering Winnicott's powerful words (1980, p63): *it is in playing and only in playing that the individual child or adult is able to be creative and to use the whole personality. It is only in being creative that the individual discovers the self.*

I hope to have convinced you that SMSC is not something tangential, to be dealt with only in certain lessons or through setting up a specific programme. Remember that:

- **spiritual experience can occur at any time;**
- **every action can be seen in moral terms;**
- **social development occurs in every aspect of school life;**
- **culture affects how we all understand experience.**

Whatever we do as teachers can affect children's spiritual, moral, social and cultural development. But don't feel overwhelmed. Much of what you do without conscious thought contributes positively to children's SMSC. The next three chapters suggest what you can do, more practically and more consciously, to enrich this, starting with how to create an environment which enhances children's spiritual, moral, social and cultural experience.

Recommended reading

Claxton, G (1997) *Hare brain, tortoise mind: why intelligence increases when you think less.* London: Fourth Estate. A good read, which highlights that deep learning relies on reflection and slowing down rather than just focus and concentration.

Gardner, H (1993) *Frames of Mind: the Theory of Multiple Intelligences.* London: Fontana. An influential, well-written book which has broadened many people's view of intelligence and how we should value the whole range of abilities in all children.

Winnicott, D (1980) *Playing and Reality.* London: Penguin. A famous psychoanalyst's study of play and infancy, which provides a wonderful, life-changing read, especially for those interested in young children.

Other references

Bruner J and Haste, H (1987) *Making Sense: the child's construction of the world.* London: Methuen

Bruner, J (1996) *The Culture of Education.* Cambridge, MA: Harvard University Press

Claxton, G (2002) *BLP: Building Learning Power.* Bristol: TLO Ltd.

Donaldson, M (1984) *Children's Minds.* London: Flamingo

Donaldson, M (1992) *Human Minds: an exploration.* London: Penguin

Hay, D with Nye, R (1998) *The Spirit of the Child.* London: Fount

Herman, JL (2001) *Trauma and Recovery: From Domestic Abuse to Political Terror.* London: Pandora

Kimes Myers, B (1997) *Young Children and Spirituality.* London: Routledge

Krog, A. (1998) *Country of My Skull.* London: Vintage

Lewis, J (2000) Spiritual Education in the Cultivation of Qualities of the Heart and Mind: A Reply to Blake and Carr in *Oxford Review of Education* vol. 26 no. 2 pp. 263-83

Macintyre, A (1999) *After Virtue.* London: Duckworth

Ofsted (2005) *Healthy Minds: Promoting emotional health and well being in schools* www.ofsted.gov.uk publication 2457

Pollard, A (1985) *The Social World of the Primary School.* London: Cassell

Timimi, S (2005) *Naughty Boys.* Basingstoke: Palgrave Macmillan

Vygotsky, L (1978) *Mind in Society: the development of higher psychological processes.* Cambridge, MA: Harvard University Press

Winterson, J (1996) *Oranges Are Not the Only Fruit.* London: Vintage

Young, RM (1994) *Mental Space.* London: Process Press

7 CREATING ENVIRONMENTS TO ENCOURAGE SPIRITUAL, MORAL, SOCIAL AND CULTURAL DEVELOPMENT

By the end of this chapter you should:

- *understand why ethos and environment are so important in SMSC;*
- *have thought about the features of an environment conducive to SMSC;*
- *have considered dilemmas in creating an environment designed to enhance SMSC within the current context;*
- *recognise that SMSC depends more on how you teach than what you teach.*

This will help you to meet Standards:
→ *S 1.1, 1.2, 1.3, 1.5, 2.2, 2.4, 2.7, 3.2.4, 3.3.1, 3.3.8, 3.3.9, 3.3.14*

I hope that the previous six chapters have stimulated you to think about SMSC and personal development rather differently. You may be wondering what this means in practice and how it fits in with competing demands on your time. The next three chapters are designed to help you think, and feel confident, about making provision likely to offer the types of experience and develop qualities associated with SMSC. In this chapter, we consider ethos and environment, in Chapter 8 the craft of teaching and in Chapter 9 the formal curriculum and planning. As you read them and as you teach, it is worth considering:

- **What sorts of experiences help to develop or enhance the qualities associated with SMSC?**

- **Are these the same for all children?**

- **What can, and can't, you do to enhance children's SMSC?**

Here are three bits of good news. First, much of what teachers do in the normal course of teaching contributes positively to SMSC. Second, good provision for SMSC depends more on the environment and ethos created than new activities, or assessment procedures, or plans. Third, the overlap between the four elements of SMSC means that a similar environment tends to be suitable for all of them.

What do ethos and environment mean?

The curriculum is often considered as having three aspects: **formal**, **informal** and **hidden**. Broadly speaking, the formal curriculum refers to planned, intended activities, such as lessons and assemblies, and overt statements, such as rules and procedures. The informal curriculum involves what happens around the school, on the playground and optional activities. The hidden curriculum relates to implicit aspects of school life, such as values and expectations, relationships and responses. It will be no surprise that SMSC can occur in all three, but especially in the hidden curriculum, described by the term 'ethos'.

A school's ethos is something you can feel, like a climate or an atmosphere, but even experienced teachers find it hard to pin down in words. Strangely, it is easier for an outsider, such as an inspector or parent, to describe than for someone who works there all the time. Familiarity tends to make us take such things for granted. I recall the struggle of one deputy head to describe his school's ethos, although the notices, visual displays and noise level gave me a strong sense within five minutes of what it was like to teach or learn there. Formal statements of intent matter less than what actually happens, which is best captured through examples:

- explicit assertions of values, such as the cross prominent in most Catholic schools or what children wear;
- visible but usually less consciously chosen aspects, such as how children are praised or punished, the welcome to visitors or the amount of litter; and
- implicit aspects, such as how children move around the school, how adults talk to children and small actions such as holding doors open.

Think of a school you have visited on school experience.

- **What sort of learning environment was it?**
- **What values were expressed and how?**
- **Which specific features are conducive to children's SMSC?**

In Chapter 3, I introduced the idea of schools as 'moral communities', referring to Jackson et al. (1993)'s research presenting every aspect of school life as having a moral basis. Every feature of an environment influences moral – and by extension spiritual, social and cultural – development, from the smile for a child arriving at school for the first time to the final assembly as that same child leaves several years later. Creating this depends on the relationships which teachers form, the example they set, and the values they demonstrate both explicitly and more subtly. SMSC is woven into the whole fabric of school life and children's learning, reaching way beyond the formal curriculum.

How a physical environment can indicate values and ethos

The physical environment often indicates the values of a school or classroom, though the most run-down building can become a wonderful learning environment and the best designed building feel harsh and unwelcoming. Simple things may contribute to SMSC, for example, creating spaces for reflection in the school grounds, such as a quiet garden or a nature area, or encouraging children to exercise their imagination by providing equipment or playground marking which encourage them to be inventive. In the classroom, this might entail displaying pictures, which celebrate cultural diversity, presenting classroom rules positively, or providing flowers or music. How you set out your classroom, the images and symbols you put up, the types of work (and whose) displayed and how the furniture is arranged expresses your values, visibly and often unconsciously. Taking care to make your classroom interesting and welcoming is time well spent.

Points for consideration and discussion

What visible features of your classroom may enhance SMSC?

Which of these reflect what you, personally, think to be important?

How much does it matter whether the children consciously notice these?

The informal and hidden curriculum is particularly significant when children are in the playground and at lunchtime. Do not assume that most children enjoy such times when structure and adult support is loosest. Conflicting expectations – from informal peer group pressures, school rules and the demands of different adults – may be confusing. Many, especially very young, children and those who find it hard to make friends, are unsure what to do. Often no familiar, trusted adult is available for support. Unsurprisingly, it is when bullying occurs most frequently, when anti-social or aggressive behaviour may be reinforced and when isolated children feel most excluded. The start of the afternoon often involves adults having to resolve disputes or help children to calm down. A brief session of quiet or enjoyable activity can often help to re-establish the right mood.

A difficult balance needs to be struck. A looser structure may help children develop qualities such as resilience and resourcefulness, learn how to make friends and exercise their imagination. But no child should have to put up with bullying and loneliness without adult support. When individual children are finding life difficult on the playground, you may have to discuss concerns with senior colleagues, and possibly to involve parents, both to say that you are aware of problems and to decide how to work together. While, therefore, playtimes and lunchtimes offer many positive opportunities, take notice of what happens out of the classroom, especially when this affects the learning environment.

Points for consideration and discussion

Why are adult expectations so important?

Does consistency mean responding exactly the same to everyone?

Which sorts of behaviour are non-negotiable?

Why are ethos and environment so important in SMSC?

It may seem, initially, obvious why a positive ethos enhances SMSC. Surely, a calm atmosphere is almost bound to lead to improved social development, one which celebrates diversity to benefit cultural development? However, the reasons run somewhat deeper.

In Chapter 6, I cited, approvingly, Pollard's idea that each of us develops a concept of 'self' by interpreting the responses of other people to our actions and that this is continually refined, providing the basis for thought and behaviour. This concept, or narrative, of self, both influences one's own responses and is constantly influenced by those of other people. Since coherent personal narratives are actively created on the basis of previous experience and changed in the light of new experience, children's beliefs about themselves and their aspirations are closely linked. If Aisha thinks she cannot read, she is less likely to become a fluent reader. Similarly, if Harry believes he is good at model-making, or cooking, or making friends, this aspiration is more likely to be self-fulfilling, unless it is unrealistic. So children's aspirations help, or hinder them, in who they become, especially in terms of their self-image. These are strongly influenced by adult expectations. Adult expectations and responses help to form the child's identity and so help children to become, in Goodman's memorable phase, 'worldmakers'. He continues (1978, p6), *worldmaking ... always starts from worlds already on hand: the making is a remaking*. Cultural norms and parental expectations may provide the seed-bed for success or may limit this by being insufficiently ambitions, or unattainably high. You can help to match children's aspirations to what can be achieved through the experience and expectations you provide, reinforcing or compensating for other influences. So, the example you offer, the experiences you present and the responses you make all contribute to the child's sense of self.

In discussing moral and social development, I emphasised that children live in a world full of confusing expectations, often because they are inconsistent and either not clear enough or too inflexible. We have seen how children learn from adults modelling appropriate responses and relationships. A structure which is both consistent and responsive to individual need is especially important in helping children develop a sense of self to guide their actions and reflect on their values, based on intrinsic motivation.

Consistency is usually considered as responding the same to everyone, with procedures designed to minimise the role of personal judgment. Policies on health and safety or child protection have to be fairly inflexible and you must find out about these early on and report concerns to senior colleagues. However, good whole-school policies on areas such as behaviour or equal opportunity indicate what response is normally appropriate and provide some leeway for professional judgment, not a one-size-fits-all approach. Children need consistency, but for a teacher to respond appropriately to individual concerns or circumstances often calls for flexibility. Take the example of racist abuse. I do not think that schools should tolerate this but how adults respond may vary. For example, the response appropriate for a five year old using a word he doesn't fully understand is surely different from that for a ten year old who knows how hurtful such a name can be. One great joy of teaching in primary schools is that responses can be based on a considerable knowledge of the individual. This helps you to be on the side of, and often literally beside, the child who is finding things tough.

An appropriate environment helps children develop the protective and transformational qualities which help to enhance SMSC. It must offer security, without being overprotective or intrusive. For example, too much adult support may stop children from becoming resilient and resourceful and children need space to become more reflective. While young children are inexperienced learners, their curiosity and openness, their enthusiasm and lack of inhibition can enable them to ask questions and to make links, unconstrained by subject boundaries and received wisdom. However, it is easy for the teacher to inhibit or discourage these, whether by being too authoritative or leaving little space for creativity, imagination or 'not-knowing'. The qualities you exemplify indicate to children which qualities to show and which to keep hidden, both consciously and implicitly in your smallest response.

How do children's needs influence what makes for a good learning environment?

Children's learning needs should be paramount in planning a good learning environment. While this sounds, and should be, obvious, a formal curriculum which concentrates on literacy and numeracy and measurable outcomes may result in too narrow a focus. Of course, many features which contribute to SMSC will be widely agreed as part of any good learning environment. However, looking at children's learning through the lens of SMSC emphasises:

- **emotional nurture as well as intellectual challenge;**
- **flexibility as well as structure;**
- **enactive and iconic, as well as symbolic, learning; and**
- **space for reflection and creativity as well as pace and skills.**

One implication of Maslow's hierarchy of needs, outlined in Chapter 4, is that emotional worries always takes priority over other needs and, unless dealt with, are likely to hinder learning. All children, at some time, have specific emotional needs, many of them deep-seated. Since learning involves challenge, going beyond one's present level of understanding, teachers are rightly expected to provide challenging activities. While children usually thrive on challenge, especially in academic learning, too much leads to confusion and disengagement and for many children a spiral of conflict and trouble. At that point, they need nurture, or hospitable space, not more challenge or confrontation.

Case study

The Art Room – combining nurture and challenge

The Art Room is a small, well-staffed unit in Oxford for children from local primary and secondary schools who find it hard to engage in mainstream school because of their emotional difficulties. Some exhibit aggressive behaviour, while others are very quiet. Most have very troubled backgrounds and lack the internal resources to regulate their behaviour appropriately. At the Art Room children do a range of artistic activities, including drawing, painting and making models, mostly individual, such as portraits, but some collective, such as big collages. The environment is very welcoming, with comfortable chairs and food. What is really remarkable is the combination of consistent expectations, clearly set out as positive rules, and the willingness to help children to understand these and to deal with their emotional responses, which otherwise result in anxiety or anger.

The staff's ability to model appropriate responses and not to be provoked is essential. This brings remarkable benefits in just a few weeks, especially with primary-age children who are less likely to have become very disaffected.

You may, reasonably, say that the Art Room's approach is impossible in an ordinary classroom. But it demonstrates that nurturing does not involve accepting any behaviour, which helps neither the child nor the rest of the class. Usually, positive affirmation of what other children are doing, especially with younger children, or reference to class rules will be enough. But when a child lacks the internal resources to regulate their emotions, they need support, not simply to be told to behave properly. This may be something simple and short term. For example, Kerry, a troubled ten year old, was recently complaining to me that everyone was annoying her when the reverse seemed to be the case. Several reprimands to her and to other children were ineffective. But a few minutes of sitting with her to offer individual attention helped her get out of a spiral of provocation and response, at least for a while. However, emotional nurture may require more long-term and demanding support, as in this story...

Case study

The boy who loved everything to be ordered

Jonah was seven when he came to our school. Originally from Africa, he had spent several months out of school for reasons we never established. He was very wary of adults and children. Initially, he flew into almost uncontrollable tantrums, becoming a danger to other children and sometimes the teacher. Soon, after a period of close adult attention, to ensure that he did not disrupt or hurt other children or run away, he would happily settle to a very structured activity, such as completing a puzzle or colouring a picture. He loved everything to be 'just right' and at the end of school would empty his rucksack and painstakingly re-pack it until it met his requirements. After two or three months, he could cope with a less tightly controlled structure and more choice, blossoming into a warm, affectionate and happy boy.

Points for consideration and discussion

How can one provide nurture as well as challenge in a busy classroom?

What sorts of activities encourage children to use different modes of learning?

What are the implications for your classroom environment?

In Chapter 3, I discussed Bruner's distinction between enactive, iconic and symbolic modes of learning. Language is vital in SMSC as in other learning, for example to develop the higher-order concepts which enable reflection on the qualities necessary for SMSC. A child's narrative is, at least in part, described and elaborated through the use of words. However, for teachers to rely too much on language limits young children's learning repertoire, especially in the early years. In Sunderland's words

(2000, p2), *everyday language is not the natural language of feeling for children. Their natural language is that of image and metaphor, as in stories and dreams.* Since under-standing and memory often precede, and can bypass, language, making use of enactive and visual modes is, and remains, essential in deep learning. Adults, who tend to assume that learning occurs mainly through language, may find this hard to grasp, but its implications are profound.

Much experience which enhances SMSC engages enactive and iconic modes of learn-ing. Enactive learning might entail acting out a story in RE or designing and conducting an experiment in science, as well as more obvious opportunities in PE or constructing a tall tower. Visual, or iconic, learning reaches far beyond having the chance to appreciate art, be critical of the values expressed in an advert or become 'film-literate', important as these are. Learning how to relate to unfamiliar people or appreciating the complexity of the pattern on a butterfly's wing depends heavily on visual learning rather than simply conscious processes.

Direct, first-hand experience provides a route into deep personal learning, largely because it stimulates an emotional as well as a linguistic-cognitive response. The younger the child, the greater the reliance on enactive and visual modes of learning, but all children (and adults) learn at the deepest level by using these parts of the learning repertoire. For example, remember how play enables children to imagine themselves as someone different, often without conscious thought. And looking closely at, or drawing, a natural object such as a shell, or examining in detail an arte-fact such as a sarcophagus from Ancient Egypt, can help children to understand where they fit into the wider scheme of things or gain some awareness of what it was like to live under the Pharaohs. Such experience provides opportunities for wonder and mystery, encouraging a sense of perspective and empathy.

Learning styles

The well-known idea of different learning styles reflects, in part, Bruner's work. Put simply, this suggests that everyone has one of three preferred learning styles (often shortened to VAK):

- **visual;**
- **auditory;**
- **kinaesthetic.**

This is useful in so far as it reminds teachers that learning occurs in different ways and that most learning is likely to be enhanced by varied means of presentation. However, there is a danger that, if one labels a child as one sort of learner, the teacher does not develop their full range of learning modes and styles. This is like discouraging someone good at drawing from developing other artistic talents or saying to a child who loves fiction not to bother with non-fiction. Try to present activities in ways that encourage children to use different approaches to learning, but be careful not to assume that individuals have only one, as opposed to a preferred, learning style.

A breadth of experience which draws on, and develops, different modes of learning helps children's search for a coherent narrative and a mature identity. So, a focus on language and skills should be balanced with activities and experiences that release and encourage children's creativity and develop the whole range of intelligences. This is valuable for all children, but especially so for some. For example, it provides alternative routes into learning for those who find listening hard – whether the many young children with some, often temporary, hearing loss or those unused to concentrating for long periods. A broad range of experience and learning modes both reduces reliance on prior knowledge and experience, which the same children may lack, and is likely to help develop appropriate language.

SMSC tends to emphasise search and questions, space and enabling because creating a coherent personal narrative is an active process, requiring critical judgment and chances for reflection rather than imposition. Piaget's view (in Papert, 1999) that *children have real understanding only of that which they invent themselves and each time that we try to teach them something too quickly, we keep them from reinventing themselves* is as true of personal identity as other learning. Children need time and opportunities to puzzle over questions with no easy or definitive answers and to envisage how they might become who they would wish to be. This requires an environment that does not overemphasise the immediate and the short term and allows for questions that cannot be answered definitively. Unless children are allowed, encouraged and empowered to ask questions and explore uncertainties, whether silently or out loud, their sense of themselves as active enquirers is inhibited. A learning environment conducive to SMSC needs to allow, to enable and to invite, not simply to instruct.

Case study

Spiders' webs on an autumn day

A few weeks into my first year of teaching Year 2 children, there was a glorious autumn morning with droplets of water glistening on spiders' webs in the school hedge. I took the class out to look at and talk about this. We went in after ten minutes or so and carried on with the lesson. Shortly afterwards, I noticed that Emma, a child who had barely spoken and found most learning very difficult, was not there. I found her outside, on her own, still looking at the webs. Asked why, she just said 'They're so beautiful.' I left her there, but kept an eye on her through the window, until she came in shortly afterwards. I judged this to be a moment of significance, not to be interrupted – do you remember the teacher who loved biology because, as a child, he had looked down into rock pools?

Points for consideration and discussion

Should I have taken the class out?

How would you have responded to Emma?

What, if anything, do you think that Emma gained from the experience?

Every parent and teacher will agree with the emphasis in *Every Child Matters* (Children Act, 2004) that is placed on a safe environment. A good environment for learning helps children both to feel safe and to practise and develop appropriate responses. For example, I referred, in Chapter 4, to how mood affects how emotion is experienced and regulated. An individual's mood is strongly influenced by immediate relationships and the social environment. A climate of support or hostility affects how we respond to emotions as varied as joy or anxiety, anger or surprise. An appropriate mood helps all children (and adults) to regulate their emotions and responses, though this is of particular benefit to the vulnerable.

Policies, procedures and rules all help provide a structure within which both children and adults feel safe. Yet creative learning, which is fundamental to cultural and spiritual development, involves a level of risk. This will vary with the age and experience of the children, the group size and the mood of a class or teacher. To deny children the chance to make mistakes is to restrict their learning. As a teacher, you have a responsibility to minimise the risk of physical harm, such as using scissors with young children or tools in design technology in Key Stage 2. Team sport entails some danger of getting hurt. Such situations need to be managed carefully, and policies are in place to help this. Similar considerations apply to emotional safety. We overprotect children if we deny them the chance to explore their emotions and enable them to develop qualities such as creativity, imagination and playfulness, by allowing an element of managed risk.

Points for consideration and discussion

How can you provide breadth of experience and space for reflection in your classroom?

How will this affect how you teach a class of 5 year olds? Or 10 year olds?

How does the ethos and environment of the school affect you as a classroom teacher?

How does the whole-school ethos affect you as a class teacher?

Schools vary enormously both in the importance they ascribe to SMSC and how they approach it. The school is part of a wider system with various groups having different, often conflicting, demands and expectations. Among these are:

- national government and organisations such as Ofsted;
- local authorities and groups such as diocesan authorities in Church schools;
- the local community, both through the governors and directly from parents;
- the staff who work in the school.

The headteacher has to take account of, and balance, these different groups.

Just as a child's SMSC is enhanced, or hindered, by the environment you create, your own provision is affected by many whole-school factors, including the school's values and beliefs, curriculum policies and expectations and social and cultural beliefs in the local community. These will influence both your children's SMSC and how you teach – and how much you enjoy teaching. For example, teaching in a Church school will probably result in you being expected to promote Christian values. A village school may expect you to take part in activities that extend your professional life beyond school time. A school with poor academic results may present fewer opportunities for encouraging children's creativity. You may be very happy with these expectations, or not, but you will have to take account of them in your provision for SMSC.

The whole-school ethos can encourage, or restrict, you as a teacher, just as you can your children. For example, reports and guidance such as *All our Futures* (NACCCE, 1999), Ofsted (2003) and *Excellence and Enjoyment* (DfES, 2003) all call for teaching for creativity. It is hard to be against this, at least in theory. But many teachers are, in practice, wary of activities which encourage creativity, because they tend to be messier and noisier, and may be harder to control and not lead to outcomes which are easily assessed or measured. When teachers are being monitored or inspected, there is every temptation to play safe. So, a headteacher and a school culture which encourages trying out new approaches and sees mistakes as opportunities for learning rather than for disapproval can make all the difference between you being prepared to have a go and choosing the cautious option – however much children may benefit from the former.

Your school may have a whole-school programme to develop emotional literacy and personal development, such as Values Education or Family Links, or approaches based on the SEAL (Social and Emotional Aspects of Learning) materials (see SEBS in the references). Most aim to create a nurturing environment throughout the school to help children regulate their emotional responses. This can be extremely helpful, for both adults and children, as long as they are combined with 'walking the talk', though they:

- **need the commitment from senior staff, especially the head, and so can get messy without regular refreshment and training;**
- **can overemphasise the role of language in making choices, when some children's background and emotional resources make it hard for them to articulate their feelings and possible strategies in words;**
- **may, ironically, focus so much on emotional literacy and behaviour that schools do not provide the intellectual challenge which all children also need.**

If you are lucky enough to work in a school committed to meeting emotional needs, whether through a formal programme or not, this really helps you as a classroom teacher. If not, it is harder but not impossible to make good provision for SMSC.

You can influence and contribute to the whole-school ethos more than you think. Remember that you will bring new ideas, especially having read this book! When asked, be prepared to offer your views on school policies and approaches, for example in the process of school self-evaluation. You will probably find that your suggestions will be welcomed. Even if not, or you are not in sympathy with the school's philosophy and approach, you may be surprised how much you can contribute to, and shape, this. But avoid being too direct, working more through how you speak, and listen, to children, the work which you display, the visits which you plan. You can certainly make a big difference in your own classroom by the values you espouse, the activities you set up, the expectations you have, the responses you make, the language you use, the sensitivity and respect you show for children's backgrounds. Where these are not well established, you can, over time, start to shift a school's approach. In any case, they are worthwhile in themselves and your children will benefit.

How can teachers resolve the dilemmas in creating a classroom environment conducive to SMSC?

Your course, and most guidance to teachers, will focus on the formal curriculum, highlighting the content of what children should learn and an approach full of pace and challenge, with a strong focus on explicit learning, classroom management and measurable outcomes. Important as these are, much learning associated with SMSC is less conscious and intentional, with outcomes to do with personal qualities such as empathy or imagination, or greater awareness of one's own place within a society or a culture, rarely open to measurement. An appropriate environment for SMSC draws on children's existing capacity for these and enables them to be developed further.

This chapter has highlighted several dilemmas in how to create an environment sensitive to children's needs in relation to SMSC, in a culture with a strong emphasis on challenge and pace, on instruction and skills and on language. In working out how to resolve these dilemmas, remember that:

- **these are not either/or, but aspects of children's learning to be balanced;**
- **good provision for SMSC may entail setting up specific activities or experiences, but more often it involves steering activities slightly differently;**
- **although these ideas are complicated, they can help you decide how to approach your teaching in the classroom tomorrow or next week.**

Your plans and responses will have to take account of the many variables in any school or classroom. I can only offer pointers to help you make the judgments appropriate to a specific time and context. This calls for a pedagogy more thoughtful and flexible than just downloading lessons from the internet or finding activities in a book of resources. If you want specific activities, the list of recommended reading below includes two useful books and I shall in Chapter 9 suggest other sources. Such resources can be useful, but enhancing children's SMSC involves engaging with the complexity of children's lives and learning. The term 'pedagogy' is used more in central Europe than in England to indicate the complexity of the whole craft of teaching. Levine (Meek, 1996, p96) described pedagogy as *that complex of thinking, feeling, information, knowledge, theory, experience, wisdom and creativity which are the inherent, acquired and continuously-honed qualities of individual good teachers.* Pedagogy covers every aspect of teaching, reflecting the complexity of the teacher's role that can be lost if teachers are seen only as deliverers or technicians.

Much of the pedagogy which enhances SMSC often entails approaching what is familiar from a different perspective and involves such apparently small actions as:

- **attending to your children and responding to their concerns, especially at points of vulnerability;**
- **enjoying their company, celebrating their successes and sharing their pleasures;**
- **demonstrating how to regulate one's emotions and interact with other people;**
- **helping children to appreciate the simple things of life, from a funny incident to a thoughtful comment or action.**

As well as the content of the National Curriculum and school schemes of work, good teaching, especially in relation to SMSC, focuses on the *how* of children's learning and teachers teaching more than the *what*. In the next chapter we explore more of the detail of what a pedagogy to enhance SMSC looks like.

Recommended reading

Dowling, M (2000) *Young Children's Personal, Social and Emotional Development.* London: Paul Chapman Publishing. Practical and accessible, with many ideas for enhancing PSE for children in the early years.

Norman, S (2003) *Transforming Learning – Introducing SEAL Approaches.* London: Saffire. Short illuminating descriptions of different approaches designed to enhance children's learning by accessing untapped elements of the brain's capacity – but do not believe the claims made for all of them.

SEBS Social, Emotional and Behavioural Skills www.teachernet.gov.uk/teachingandlearning/socialandpastoral/sebsl

Other references

Children Act (2004) see www.everychildmatters.gov.uk/ete/primaryschool

DfES (Department for Education and Skills) (2003) *Excellence and enjoyment: a strategy for primary schools.* Nottingham: DfES

Goodman, N (1978) *Ways of Worldmaking.* Hassocks: Harvester

Jackson, PW, Boostrom, RE, and Hansen, DT (1993) *The Moral Life of Schools.* San Francisco, CA: Jossey Bass

Meek, M (ed.) (1996) *Developing Pedagogies in the Multilingual Classroom – the writings of Josie Levine.* Stoke on Trent: Trentham Books

NACCCE (National Advisory Committee on Creative and Cultural Education) (1999) *All Our Futures: Creativity, Culture and Education.* London: DfEE

Ofsted (2003) *Expecting the unexpected – developing creativity in primary and secondary schools.* www.ofsted.gov.uk/publications HMI 1612

Papert, S (1999) www.papert.org/articles/papertonpiaget – accessed 17 March 2006

Sunderland, M (2000) *Using Storytelling as a Therapeutic Tool with Children.* Bicester: Winslow Press

8 APPROACHING SPIRITUAL, MORAL, SOCIAL AND CULTURAL DEVELOPMENT IN THE CLASSROOM

By the end of this chapter you should:

- *have a clearer understanding of pedagogical approaches which enhance SMSC;*
- *have considered how to adapt your teaching to take account of children's SMSC;*
- *understand the place of summative assessment, especially in reporting to parents and the close link between formative assessment and teaching;*
- *recognise the importance of how children are grouped;*
- *have reflected on the use of language and gesture.*

This will help you to meet Standards:
➔ *S 1.1, 1.2, 1.3, 1.5, 1.6, 1.7, 2.4, 2.7, 3.1.1, 3.1.2, 3.1.3, 3.2.1, 3.2.2, 3.2.3, 3.2.4, 3.3.1, 3.3.4, 3.3.6, 3.3.7, 3.3.9, 3.3.14*

Good provision for SMSC is woven into the fabric of school life and the learning environment created, rather than pigeon-holed into any one subject or compartmentalised into separate lessons or experiences. To illustrate how your pedagogy can be enriched by taking account of SMSC, and how to enhance SMSC, I consider, in this chapter, four familiar aspects: assessment, differentiation, target-setting and language and gesture. But I start with three examples – of an assembly, an incident in the home corner and a story – to illustrate features of good provision for SMSC. As you read them, think about the following questions. As before, discuss these in a group if you can. Think how, if at all, the following examples:

- **show the adult assessing children's abilities?**
- **indicate different expectations according to this assessment?**
- **demonstrate the link between adult expectations and children's actions?**
- **highlight teaching approaches which draw on different learning modes?**

Case study

A memorable assembly

Of all the assemblies that I have watched, one sticks in my mind. The whole school, about eighty children, settled calmly, listening to music, with the head at the front, and a candle, a stone and some twisted barbed wire on a table. He greeted everyone and introduced the theme of people in trouble because of their beliefs. He asked everyone to pair up to discuss what they believed to be really important, with older children moving to talk with younger one and adults present joining in. After two minutes or so, volunteers offered some examples, on which he drew to indicate why some people around the world were imprisoned unjustly, mentioning the barbed wire as Amnesty's symbol.

The assembly ended with a minute's silence, then music again. All over within fifteen minutes, but a chance for quiet, thoughtful discussion, at the child's level, a simple message and a time of reflection. An oasis of calm in a busy day.

Points for consideration and discussion

Which types of experiences or qualities in SMSC was this likely to enhance?

What had the head prepared in advance to create the right atmosphere?

What can the class teacher learn from this?

In primary schools, especially, collective worship, commonly thought of as assembly, offers many possibilities in relation to SMSC. 'Collective' recognises that those present may not all share a religious belief. For the whole school, or one section, to gather enables each child to see themselves as part of a bigger entity. The person leading the assembly can reaffirm positive values, maybe with a story, using a symbol such as a candle or a flower, or celebrating the successes of individuals or groups. The chance to reflect together, with silence, music or a prayer, affirms the importance of taking a break from the busy-ness of life to ponder questions of deeper significance. Note how the head enabled the children's participation by asking for their ideas, encouraging discussion and drawing on their responses.

Case study

An incident in the home corner

In a class of four and five year olds, I observed Ruth, a quiet, timid girl, approaching and apparently wishing to enter the home corner which was dominated by some boys playing noisily. She hesitated and watched, for several seconds, before seeking the help of the nursery nurse who told her to go back and say that Mrs H had said that she (Ruth) can play in the house. Ruth went back and looked into the playhouse, for about forty-five seconds, apparently impassive but keen to go in. As she approached she smiled, and looked back, presumably for reassurance, at Mrs H, who was watching. Ruth returned and said that the boys were playing dinosaurs. The nursery nurse said 'Go and say Mrs H says you can play in there – and the house is for everyone.' Ruth looked doubtful but went back with two other girls. They held hands, waited for two or three seconds and then went in together. Although they did not stay long, a threshold, both literal and metaphorical, appeared to have been crossed.

Points for consideration and discussion

What sort of experience was this for Ruth? What qualities were enhanced?

What did the nursery nurse do to enable this?

How might she have acted differently? What would the likely result have been?

This incident demonstrates an adult intervening at just the right level, scaffolding, supporting and encouraging Ruth, but enabling her – and so building her confidence and resilience. This required an assessment, based on experience, a judgment of what the child was capable of, in that context, and an expectation of her to do more than she herself believed that she could – all backed by the adult's attention to her own language and gestures and Ruth's response.

Case study

Handa's Surprise – a simple story?

I watched a skilled teacher of four and five year olds reading the story, Handa's Surprise, *about an African girl, carrying on her head a basket of fruit, the contents of which keep changing without her knowledge, as various animals remove pieces of fruit. Both the story and the subsequent discussion operated at several levels, evoking excitement and humour, encouraging the children to think what the girl could see, and why she was unaware of what was happening, presenting issues about morality, intention and values, and helping children to learn about unfamiliar fruit and culture. The teacher discussed with me why she had chosen the story and concentrated on specific aspects. Most obvious was counting and listing what was in the basket. However, she commented on the moral dilemmas, which she did not highlight, but was prepared to discuss if raised by a child and might refer to them subsequently. More subtly, she had chosen the story to illustrate cultural diversity but did not point that out specifically, preferring to let the message operate subconsciously.*

Points for consideration and discussion

Was the teacher right not to make explicit every aspect she had considered? Why?

What might the children have gained that relates to SMSC?

Why is story so valuable in enhancing SMSC?

On the face of it, this looks to be simple incident of a teacher reading a story. However, both the story chosen and how it was read raise questions related to each of the four elements of SMSC. The teacher had anticipated many possibilities but did not make all of these explicit. Reliance only on the children's ideas makes it unlikely that the deeper levels will be uncovered, but using only those that the teacher had planned is unlikely to engage the children as active interpreters. Individual children could engage with the story at different levels, within a group. Since all the possibilities for SMSC are never foreseeable, a good environment for learning is always being recreated in the moment.

What is the role of assessment in SMSC?

Ofsted (2004, p27) states that *the starting point [in evaluating SMSC] is how well the school provides an environment in which pupils' spiritual, moral, social and cultural development can flourish*, making no mention of levels or scores. So, you must learn to live without the (often rather superficial) certainty that numbers offer. Trying to measure the outcomes associated with personal development, and placing children on levels, is totally inappropriate. The most important aspects of education will always remain beyond measurement. Moreover, an emphasis on scores often narrows the range of expectations and what is taught.

Let us distinguish between two types of assessment:

- **summative, evaluating what has been done;**
- **formative, looking at the current situation, to decide what to do next.**

Good provision for SMSC depends on formative assessment, often called assessment for learning, to help you work out what children will benefit from based on their prior experience. However, summative assessment has its place in SMSC, especially when discussing individual children with parents and other colleagues and when considering how successful your provision has been.

Parent consultations and end of year reports are the most obvious times for summative assessment of SMSC, looking back over a period of several weeks or months. Parents are likely to be at least as interested in your comments on their children's personal development as in academic results, especially with younger children. Remember that SMSC is one area where almost all parents have knowledge you may find useful, often including aspects of which you may have no idea. Try to see discussions with parents, whether at parents' evenings or informally at the classroom door, as a chance for you to learn as well to inform and to decide on how best to enhance personal development (probably without using the language of SMSC). So, asking questions, especially when you are genuinely puzzled, is often more productive than providing definite answers. Since time is often short, you may have to raise such questions. Similarly, the space to discuss personal development on end of year reports is usually tiny. I always had far too much to say to fit in a small box! Although you will want to maintain good relationships with parents, keeping some distance helps when you have to give difficult messages or defend what is unpopular. While you need to be honest, remember how sensitive and personal such matters may be, with parents often feeling open to criticism. Ask a senior member of staff to join you, especially when you have difficult things to say. And remember to suggest positive ways forward and not to leave the awkward bits till the end.

Summative assessment of SMSC provision is likely to happen when reviewing how children have responded to specific planned experiences, such as a visit to a synagogue or looking after the school grounds; or whether opportunities identified in short-term plans came to fruition and how these can be extended or new opportunities created in future planning. Once one worries less about scores and levels, the distinction between summative and formative assessment becomes less sharp. I have emphasised the importance of feedback in how we learn. Formative assessment also involves 'feedforward' – advice on what to do next, just as a doctor decides on treatment on the basis of diagnosis. Black et al. (2002) highlight that unless children know what they have to do to improve they are likely to remain confused about what to do next. Interestingly, that pamphlet, although focused mainly on secondary schools and academic attainment, emphasises similar messages to this book's, such as the emphasis on active learning, on questioning and the teacher being in control, but not too controlling.

Points for consideration and discussion

How can you assess children's needs in terms of personal development?

Should one have different expectations of boys and girls? Or children from different backgrounds?

How much should adult responses take account of such factors?

Appropriate feedback and feedforward requires knowledge of the current state of the child's understanding and previous experience. This may be relatively easy in mathematics or history, but extremely hard in relation to SMSC, calling for judgment and sensitivity to context. Making appropriate provision for SMSC depends on a sensitivity to long-term factors, such as gender, background and socio-economic background, which affect his or her sense of self and response. For example, attitudes to work, or the importance of particular values, may be heavily influenced by family background. However, assuming that boys, or the daughters of professors, or children of Bangladeshi heritage, will act in a particular way easily leads to damaging stereotypes. So, you need to take account of such factors without assuming that these dictate how an individual child will act. This provides the basis for differentiating your provision accordingly.

However, also be aware, and take account, of the immediate situation. This comes surprisingly easily to most teachers, as long as they recognise why it matters and trust their own judgment. For example, a ten year old who explains that he is late because his house has been broken into may need to talk about this. A five year old excited about the birth of a baby sister is likely to be taken up with this, at least for a while. Sometimes, a brief recognition of these will be enough, maybe with a private comment or a class discussion, in general terms. At other times, coming to understand a child's needs in terms of SMSC takes place over a longer time, assembling details like the pieces of a mosaic, for example by:

- **paying attention to children's joys and anxieties, interests and responses, even if you do not respond immediately;**
- **looking out for when a child behaves uncharacteristically, especially over time;**
- **taking notice of changes of external circumstances, remembering that what happens outside the classroom and the school affects children's sense of self, and so their ability to learn.**

Such assessment may not result in very obvious changes to your teaching, but pedagogy to enhance SMSC often entails subtle shifts of response and sensitivity to circumstances.

What does SMSC suggest about differentiation?

Excellence and Enjoyment (DfES, 2003) called for more 'personalised' learning. Quite what this means, and its implications, remains unclear. If it involves children learning on their own with individualised learning programmes using electronic technology, it will overlook the social and relational basis of learning. If it means extending opportunities and adapting provision according to individual children's circumstances and needs, I am all for it, as primary school teachers have always recognised this as essential.

Few teachers would doubt that provision in maths, or science, or PE should be differentiated, or adapted, depending on the child's age, aptitude or prior experience. Quite what differentiation in relation to personal development entails is less obvious.

Three types of differentiation are widely recognised:

- **by task – setting different tasks usually according to age and ability;**
- **by support – giving more help to some children;**
- **by outcome – using open-ended activities to encourage different types of response.**

While it is obvious that activities contributing to SMSC will vary according to age, this is a matter of degree. Although young children benefit hugely from opportunities for play, the need for this continues in Key Stage 2 (and adulthood!), especially for those who have had insufficient opportunities when younger. While older children may benefit from specific times for reflection, those in Key Stage 1 can be introduced to this and other activities which allow space for reflection. Differentiation by task and support tend to be based on an assessment of ability and learning needs. At times, differentiation by support will be valuable, based on an assessment of:

- **individual or group need, for instance to extend cultural awareness, to offer additional opportunities for nurture or identify hidden talents;**
- **qualities such as resilience or empathy, or factors such as gender and background, for example with unassertive children or those having a hard time at home benefiting from activities which help them express their views or nurture them.**

Enhancing the qualities and values associated with SMSC calls more for differentiation by outcome and by response. The types of experience and the qualities associated with SMSC are most likely to be enhanced where children with varied abilities are engaged in open-ended, collaborative activities with a wide range of possible outcomes – differentiation by outcome. However, given the importance of reciprocity and feedback in how children learn, the differentiation which most enhances SMSC is where the response of adults and other children takes account of the individual child's own needs and responses. This differentiation by response can most directly be achieved by your own, or other adults', direct responses. However, how children are grouped also contributes to the sort of feedback they receive, but this does entail you being prepared to intervene in ways that either you or the children may find uncomfortable.

Points for consideration and discussion

Why is grouping so important in enhancing SMSC?

How much should a teacher intervene to alter children's values and attitudes?

Is it desirable to group children according to gender? Or other attributes?

Grouping is an aspect of pedagogy where SMSC reinforces some, and challenges other, current orthodoxies. For example, pair work and a plenary session are widely regarded as part of a good teacher's repertoire. Discussion in twos and threes enables children to take risks without being shown up in front of the whole group. This stimulates more active engagement than choosing one child to answer with everyone else either waiting patiently or, more likely, switching off. Alexander (2000) examines, in detail, how other countries, notably France and Russia, use collective 'thinking out loud' to encourage a greater understanding of other points of view and higher-order thinking. However, the plenary can easily become a teacher-led summary of the teacher's initial intentions rather than a discussion that explores what children have learnt and what they are unsure of. Children explaining their way of thinking to a whole class may be more effective than a teacher's explanation because they start nearer to other children's current understanding. These approaches are not specific to SMSC, but help to develop such abilities as:

- thinking 'outside the box', creatively;
- developing empathy and mutual respect;
- learning to live with difference.

In Chapter 4, I presented controversial views about boys and girls. This may raise more hackles! Since the expectations of society and of the peer group combine to affect how gender identity and aspirations are formed, stereotypical behaviour is likely to persist without specific intervention, for example by:

- grouping children deliberately by gender in ways outlined above;
- monitoring whether your questions and responses to boys and girls reflect the gender balance of the class;
- helping girls to be assertive and boys to express their emotions and have greater awareness of other people's feelings;
- encouraging both girls and boys to challenge such behaviour and aspirations in themselves and others.

Deciding to work like this may be controversial. However, unless teachers are prepared to intervene actively to counter the gender roles embedded in society and the media, these roles are likely to be reinforced, by omission.

Points for consideration and discussion

Should teachers actively encourage actions and attitudes in this way?

If so, should they do so even when parents do not agree?

If not, what other strategies can you use to avoid stereotypes being reinforced?

Looking at group work through the SMSC lens makes a strong case for children working in groups arranged depending on the intended outcome, rather than always by ability or friendship. For example:

- in **PE, I sometimes put those of similar ability together and sometimes ask them to work in mixed-ability groups;**
- in **drama, I often break up friendship groups to encourage children to become more adventurous (but it doesn't always work!);**
- in **science, I usually arrange mixed-gender groups, so that girls are encouraged to take lead roles and boys to work more collaboratively.**

Such an approach to grouping may, initially, be unpopular, often with parents. However, if children are to learn to live in a diverse society, they must learn to co-operate with unfamiliar people. As Weeks (in Mac an Ghaill, 1994, p171) writes, *all the appeals to our common interest as humans will be as naught unless we can at the same time learn to live with difference.* Putting children into unfamiliar roles has the potential to help children change their beliefs about themselves and who they can become. A much simpler reason is that those left out when children choose their own groups are nearly always the same ones – those who find it hardest to make friends and fit in anyway.

What does SMSC suggest about target-setting and learning objectives

In Chapter 7, we considered how adult expectations affect children's aspirations. Southworth, in an unpublished talk, describes how targets can make teachers' expectations explicit. Low teacher expectations are depressingly self-fulfilling, while having high expectations, sharing these with children and supporting them in meeting these, help to shape a positive sense of self.

Points for consideration and discussion

How do you make explicit your expectations?

Which of these relate to SMSC and personal development?

What is the role of individual and group targets in relation to SMSC?

A mention of targets probably makes you think of scores and percentages, especially in literacy, numeracy and national tests. The targets commonly displayed in classrooms are often skills-related and short term. It may be helpful for targets in SMSC to relate to values and personal qualities and to cover a period of several weeks. This helps both you and the children to remember the less tangible, long-term aspects of education. For example, encouraging children to be confident and imaginative, and supporting this, helps them to become so. Expecting children to persist, and guiding them, builds their resilience. Claxton's (2002) 'learning muscles,' based on sub-categories of the 4Rs, help make such expectations explicit. By emphasising one – for example, 'I want you to work really imaginatively and not to worry about getting this exactly right first time' – you make explicit the approach, or the process, rather than just the information or the skill. You may know about WALT (What I am Learning Today) and WILF (What I am Looking For) with the latter, especially, a chance to identify particular approaches and attitudes. To make some targets group-based can help emphasise interdependence, so that children think in terms of 'we', rather than a collection of 'I's. Such targets help children, individually or as a group, subsequently discuss how well they have achieved them, especially in conversation with the teacher and, where possible, other adults working alongside them.

Good learning objectives are specific in outcome, rather than descriptive of an activity, so that one can judge success. So, for example, 'learning the names of the countries of the European Union' is a learning objective, but 'looking at a map of Europe' is not. Outcomes in SMSC are rarely as short term or clear-cut as this. One solution is to have two parallel learning objectives:

- **the immediate one relating to skills to be acquired;**
- **another more process-related one, perhaps over only one lesson, perhaps over a period of a week or more.**

As an example of the latter, remember how schools involved in Values Education focus for a month on a value such as simplicity or courage.

While targets are usually public, many expectations in terms of personal development remain implicit and unspoken. Do not imagine that these are hidden from children. Even very young children understand intuitively what is approved of or otherwise. Remember the importance of adult responses for tiny babies. So, encouraging a six year old to examine really closely the pattern on a leaf may enable her to engage at a level much more profound than any teacher-led lesson. A group of ten year olds designing and constructing an electronically controlled machine useful to a disabled child is not just a good ICT activity, involving work in active citizenship and equal opportunities, but can develop qualities associated with SMSC such as imagination, creativity and empathy.

How can your language and gesture contribute to SMSC?

Language and gesture are central to the teacher's repertoire, but how they are used is crucial in enhancing SMSC. For example, your tone of voice, the words you use and your body language affect how a child acting inappropriately understands your response. In comforting a child, or sharing a moment of significance, unspoken messages, such as a touch or a smile, are just as important as overt ones. Think back to the three examples at the start of this chapter. The head's comments, actions and symbols encouraged children to vocalise their thoughts and so to elaborate their current level of understanding. The home corner incident indicated how the adult's attention and verbal and non-verbal encouragement helped the timid girl to pluck up her courage. The basket of fruit story demonstrates how the teacher, using humour, questions and comments could extend, and enrich, the children's awareness of diversity and common needs.

Points for consideration and discussion

Why are stories so valuable in making provision for SMSC?

What sort of questions help to enhance, or inhibit, children's SMSC? Why?

What actions without words contribute to a learning environment for SMSC?

Culture and identity is closely bound up with the stories handed down between generations, such as fairy tales, Greek myths, and the stories of faith, such as the Old Testament prophets and the parables, and those of the Buddha and the life of Mohammed. Or more modern figures such as Nelson Mandela and Helen Keller, and lesser-known ones such as Mary Seacole, a nurse in the Crimean War, and Raoul Wallenberg, who saved Jews from Nazi persecution. But the value of stories goes far beyond these explicit examples of good people. Most good stories contain a moral element, with which children can identify, but without explicit preaching. Indeed, one might define a good story as one which raises questions and dilemmas about how the characters should act. While most stories conclude with these in some way resolved, they leave room for imagining other possibilities.

Reading and telling good stories is an essential part of your repertoire in making provision for SMSC. Stories assist children in their search for a coherent narrative because they:

- **help children to imagine the world and themselves differently, as play does, without having to bear the emotional consequences;**
- **work at several levels simultaneously, through image and metaphor, which, as indicated, are central to how young children feel and think;**
- **provide a coherent structure for them to explore other people's feelings, beliefs, and values, and, in doing so, their own.**

Apart from these rather serious reasons, stories are enjoyable both to hear and to tell and provide a wonderful opportunity to include children of all abilities without them having to try and commit every word to memory. I will always remember how reading *The Silver Sword* over several weeks ended each day wonderfully, creating a close bond with a class of Year 5s and 6s.

There is a tremendous range of good story books relating to SMSC. The bibliography includes some used in one school where I teach. Some deal with specific issues, while others present possibilities for discussion and reflection. However, remember also the value of stories in teaching other subjects. I learnt more biology from off-beat stories than I ever did from notes. My continuing love of history results, in part, from a teacher who told wonderful stories.

Questions are especially valuable in helping children to create a coherent personal narrative when they:

- **invite the child to be active, exploratory and reciprocal;**
- **steer and guide speculation and imagination;**
- **encourage creative and divergent responses;**
- **ask their own questions, whether silently or out loud.**

I like the story of the Jewish parent who would ask his children not 'What have you learnt?' but 'Have you asked a good question today?' Open-ended questions, where there is no predetermined answer, encourage active and reflective learning. Too much certainty on the part of adults tends to constrict and close down, offering little space for mystery, paradox and ambiguity. We often do better to leave the child with further questions than to furnish answers that are not their own. So, try to avoid answering your own questions and encourage children to pause and think before anyone answers. Oakeshott's view of the link between learning and teaching is beautifully presented in Fuller (1989, pp43–62), thinking of education as a conversation between the generations.

Helping children with painful, and potentially painful, experiences

In Chapter 3, I mentioned the importance of helping children deal with painful experiences, both actual and imagined. This requires a pedagogy which is both proactive and responsive. Without being intrusive, teachers can:

- **talk about feelings of sadness, for example the death of a pet, the illness of a child in class or the memory of someone no longer at the school;**
- **explore these feelings by reading stories such as *Badger's Gift* or *Feather Pillows*;**
- **have available, especially for older children, books such as those recommended in the bibliography.**

While this cannot entirely prepare children for painful experiences when they occur, these offer emotional reference points for when painful experiences do occur. At such points, the chance to explore their feelings by thinking or drawing, by playing or talking, with a trusted adult or, where appropriate, remembering with photographs and stories, can be extremely helpful. Even more important is the sense of a trusted adult being prepared to listen and to support. Remember to be attentive but not intrusive and that it is often wise to take advice from more experienced colleagues when such occasions do occur.

This section only scratches the surface of language use. Very often, small comments are most helpful in providing feedback and encouragement to children. The nuance of how you describe a set of beliefs, 'Hindus believe', or a group, 'people who speak a language other than English' (rather than 'people who can't speak English'), or an individual who has behaved inappropriately are all parts of the fabric of pedagogy which enhances children's SMSC. What teachers do matters more than what they say, so that a laugh or a frown, an affirming nod or a pause for thought contribute – for good or ill – to the hidden curriculum which is so vital but so hard to describe. But we now turn, in the next chapter, to the formal curriculum and how to integrate SMSC across the whole curriculum.

Recommended reading

Black, P, Harrison, C, Lee, C, Marshall, B and William, D (2002) *Working inside the black box*. London: King's College. A short pamphlet, mainly related to secondary schools, with no mention of SMSC, but summarising several key points about assessment for learning.

Claxton, G (2002) *BLP: Building Learning Power*. Bristol: TLO Ltd. An accessible and practical book linking research on learning and practical ideas on how to help children 'learn to learn'.

Ofsted (2004) *Promoting and evaluating pupils' spiritual, moral, social and cultural development*. www.ofsted.gov.uk/publications. A short, easy to read summary of Ofsted's approach to SMSC and how inspectors evaluate it across the curriculum – well worth a read.

Other references

Alexander, R (2000) *Culture and Pedagogy*. Oxford: Blackwell

DfES (Department for Education and Skills) (2003) *Excellence and enjoyment: a strategy for primary schools*.

Fuller, T (ed) (1989) *Michael Oakeshott on Education*. New Haven, NJ: Yale University Press

Mac an Ghaill, M (1994) *Masculinities, Sexualities and Schooling*. Buckingham: Open University Press

9 INTEGRATING SPIRITUAL, MORAL, SOCIAL AND CULTURAL DEVELOPMENT THROUGHOUT THE CURRICULUM

By the end of this chapter you should:

- *understand the implications for planning and teaching of how SMSC crosses traditional subject boundaries;*
- *realise why some subjects offer particularly rich opportunities for SMSC;*
- *recognise opportunities for SMSC in different subject areas;*
- *have considered how to plan flexibly, incorporating SMSC into medium- and short-term planning.*

This will help you to meet Standards:

➔ *S 1.1, 1.2, 1.4, 2.1, 2.1.a, 2.1.b, 2.2, 2.4, 2.7, 3.1.1, 3.1.2, 3.2.1, 3.2.2, 3.2.6, 3.2.7, 3.3.1, 3.3.9*

How does SMSC fit in, and contribute to, a subject-based curriculum?

Ofsted (2002, p7) emphasises that, while planning and teaching in successful primary schools is largely through separate subject coverage, teachers *were adept at making good use of links across subjects*, with this:

- *strengthening the relevance and coherence of the curriculum;*
- *ensuring that pupils applied knowledge and skills in different areas, leading to greater understanding and confidence;*
- *making good use of longer blocks of times, enabling sustained work on themes covering two or three subjects.*

These considerations are especially significant in good provision for SMSC, since, as indicated in Chapter I, SMSC challenges to some extent a curriculum constructed as separate subjects. In this chapter, I discuss provision that enhances SMSC both across subject boundaries and within each subject, and highlight the subjects that offer particularly rich opportunities. I then consider the implications for medium- and short-term planning.

Treating cross-curricular themes, such as environmental awareness, equal opportunities, citizenship or SMSC, as subjects can lead to opportunities in other subject areas and throughout school life being missed. However, if not seen as a subject, with timetabled slots, they can easily be overlooked. This dilemma can be illustrated considering Personal Health and Social and Citizenship Education (PSHCE). Claire (2004) shows that the best examples of Citizenship Education occur across the curriculum and throughout school life — by children being involved in decision-making processes, learning to debate difficult issues and making a contribution to the local community. This may involve activities such as finding out information using ICT, arguing a case, writing letters and designing posters, which cut across subject boundaries.

The formal aspect of PSHCE usually contains two main elements:

- **teaching about physical health and well-being, from diet, caring for your teeth and 'stranger-danger' with children in Key Stage I, to healthy eating and drugs and sex education in Key Stage 2;**
- **developing emotional literacy, often through initiatives such as circle time to help children to talk about feelings and make appropriate choices.**

We have considered the benefits of whole-school programmes to enhance personal development through emotional literacy. Few would argue with the importance of either aspect, but these are only parts of personal development, which is not a sub-section of education but can be seen as what education is all about. Pastoral care is everyone's responsibility, throughout school life, a recognition of which makes most primary schools moral communities. We should heed Claxton's (2005, p31) sugges-tion *where possible, do your Emotional Intelligence education through the rich resources of the arts and humanities – and even in science or mathematics, through a continual acknowledgement of the role of emotion in people's lives, careers and stories.* And I would add throughout the informal and hidden curriculum.

Let us approach the same dilemma by considering two incidents:

Case study

The mystery of new life

The incubator had been in the classroom for several weeks. Although the teachers had reminded the four and five year olds every day how to be careful with, and turn, the eggs, few took much notice. One morning, I arrived to find the teachers and parents, and many of the children, very excited as the eggs had hatched. Some of the children handled the tiny chicks, others watched intently, others went off to play with a puzzle or talk to their friends. When the children gathered, the teachers discussed what had happened and during the course of the day several children, either guided to do so, or on their own, went to look at the chicks and talk about what had happened.

Points for consideration and discussion

What, if anything, was the value of this experience?

Which subject area does this fall into?

Would your answers change if this were with a class of ten year olds?

It is hard to say quite why such an experience is valuable. The children's excitement encouraged good discussion and enriched children's language. Comparison of size or questions about what had happened may have added to their mathematical and scien-tific knowledge. Drawing the chicks may have contributed to art, or the search for explanation to RE. But this does not capture something more intangible – the sense of mystery or awareness of new life such an experience is likely to have had for many of those children. With an older class, one might categorise – or test – the skills or knowledge within subject areas, but quite what any individual child had gained would remain elusive.

Case study

Becoming someone new

With a boisterous class of Year 6s, we were watching a series of programmes about the eighteenth century, with children acting different roles in small groups. Two very quiet girls rarely got animated, whatever group or role they were in. One week, I heard a tremendous commotion, with banging on the table and shouting. Curbing my natural instinct, I watched these two, suddenly transformed into peasant women refusing to be turfed out of their houses for not paying the rent. The whole class stopped, riveted. This is the power of drama, to change who one is, at least for a time. One can never know how this affected those two girls, in the longer term, but such an experience has the potential for deep and transformational learning.

Drama offers a good example of how some of the benefits of play can be incorporated into the formal curriculum with older children, such as:

• **exploring what it is like to be someone else;**
• **co-operating with others to create a new world;**
• **seeing what is familiar from another perspective.**

Engaging children at an emotional level, within a safe environment encourages creativity and imagination. While this incident occurred within history, such an approach would be possible within RE, English or geography.

Ofsted (2002, p7) describes the most successful primary schools as *[having] high standards in English, mathematics and science, while also giving a strong emphasis to the humanities, physical education and the arts.* The richness of the curriculum *contribute(s) strongly to the development of pupils' imagination and the creative use of media and materials.* This echoes my emphasis on how a breadth of experience and a balanced curriculum helps to avoid the current narrow emphasis on only two – the linguistic and logical-mathematical – of Gardner's (1993) multiple intelligences. In Key Stages 1 and 2, your timetable will almost certainly be constructed under separate subject headings, but good provision for SMSC entails working both within and across subject boundaries. Activities and experiences such as drama, experimentation and creativity which enhance personal development should not be confined to only a few subject areas.

Each subject is broken into different attainment targets (ATs), such as, in science:

• **knowledge and understanding;**
• **processes and skills;**
• **language and communication;**
• **values and attitudes.**

The emphasis is usually on the level descriptors which summarise the skills and knowledge children should have learnt at each of, usually, eight levels. However, at least one AT in each subject emphasises processes, values and attitudes. SMSC highlights the quality of the child's experience rather than the quantity of information conveyed or learnt. Enhancing this involves finding opportunities for children to develop these as well as to acquire skills and knowledge. Even quite small shifts of emphasis can help provide a curricular balance which draws on and extends the qualities contributing to children's SMSC. Despite the pressures to cover every activity in your plans or National Curriculum guidance, doing so risks superficiality with SMSC often enhanced by a slower, more thoughtful approach, with more emphasis on activity, curiosity and creativity.

In the next two sections, I consider the types of activity where SMSC is most likely to be enhanced, taking first the core, then the foundation, subjects. Listing all the activities to enhance SMSC in each subject is both impossible within the space available and inappropriate since how you, and the children, approach any activity matters more than the activity itself. For suggestions of specific activities, apart from the books recommended in Chapter 7, Appendix 5 of *Opening Windows* (Farnell et al, 2003) is very helpful, itemising in six pages:

- **questions raised;**
- **concepts, skills and attitudes;**
- **learning outcomes;**
- **things to do**

related to spiritual development. Most are, unsurprisingly, just as relevant to moral, social or cultural development. Wilson (2005) also discusses in detail how to promote creativity in different subject areas. Later in this chapter we consider how to recognise, and exploit, the opportunities and overcome the constraints specific in your own context.

Points for consideration and discussion

Which activities in English or science contribute most to personal development?

How can you develop the qualities associated with SMSC in how you present mathematics?

What approaches are likely to inhibit children's SMSC in mathematics or science?

What are the implications for the core subjects?

The opportunities to enhance SMSC in English are endless. Describing this in detail would merit a chapter of its own. Despite my belief that language is only one part of good provision for SMSC, for children to:

- **be enabled to speak confidently and listen empathetically;**
- **listen to, and make up, stories, so that they recognise other people's, and their own, questions, dilemmas and resolutions;**
- **hear poetry which, like stories, works both at an unconscious and a conscious level, leaving space for what may be puzzling, or mysterious, or exciting;**
- **read, enjoy and explore books which open up new worlds of possibility where authors explore the fundamental questions of life.**

These are among the most powerful tools for them to make sense of experience, reflect on how people should act and interact with other people, and extend their imagination and cultural awareness. We short-change them if English is reduced to handwriting, spelling and breaking texts down into their constituent parts.

Mathematics is the core subject where the opportunities for SMSC are least obvious, perhaps because it tends to focus on right answers and schemes of work are so full of content. While accuracy and pace matter, SMSC challenges an approach described by one colleague as 'motorway maths'. As in other subjects, children benefit from exploring the byways as well as driving full speed towards a destination. Specific areas where mathematics can help to enhance SMSC include:

- **exploration of 'how might this pattern develop?' or of what is hard to understand, such as infinity, leaving space for uncertainty and mystery;**
- **how mathematics has contributed inventions of great benefit or detriment to society, from the clock to the computer, the brain scanner to the bomb and the moral issues raised;**
- **the pivotal contribution of cultures such as the Babylonians, the Indians and the Arab world.**

Case study

Looking closely at moss

My Year 2 class was looking at the natural materials we had found on a woodland floor. Most concentrated on the minibeasts and leaves. However, Steven and Katie took a hand lens and examined very closely a clump of moss. They saw, and then drew, detailed drawings, remarkable mainly because they were based on accurate observation, rather than great art. I remember the intensity of the children's concentration, the depth of their enquiry, the way they examined a world of which they, and I, had previously been unaware. How can one judge the significance of such an experience? And how much does it matter if this is seen as science or art?

It is perhaps easier to see opportunities in science, since observing and interpreting what happens in the world around emphasises questions of meaning and purpose. Whether looking at materials, or forces, or the human body, science invites questions related to SMSC through methods such as prediction, observation, experiment and explanation. This may sound very grand but even watching the changing of the seasons can involve all of these. Looking at natural materials helps children to explore their place in something bigger. Numerous moral questions are raised by scientific discoveries from genetic modification to global warming. Children, once they recognise that such questions are complicated and not open to final answers, find them fascinating. While the extent to which you explore them will depend on your children's age and, perhaps, cultural background, an approach to science and technology which did not introduce its moral and social implications would be too limited.

Points for consideration and discussion

In which subject areas are enactive and iconic learning especially significant?

Which subjects encourage learning through emotional engagement?

Which subject areas deal directly with questions of personal identity?

What are the implications for the foundation subjects and RE?

While the foundation subjects, just like the core subjects, can be taught in ways that enhance, or stifle, SMSC, they have a particular role in cultivating children's creativity and imagination. It is not obvious how a dance, a rhythm or a work of art helps us learn, but they often set off processes leading to new understanding unattainable through direct instruction. For example, a class of Year 4 and 5 children looking the painting *Guernica* could see straightaway, without me guiding them, many of the themes Picasso had used. However, one reason is that they tend to encourage enactive and iconic learning. A second is that very often they engage with the learner emotionally as well as cognitively. Finally, most deal, directly or otherwise, with questions of personal identity. The foundation subjects can help to build the confidence and uncover the talents of those for whom a curriculum based on literacy and numeracy is too restrictive. This makes it worrying how little time many schools allocate to the foundation subjects, especially in Key Stage 2.

Both history and geography for very young children involve exploring how they, individually and as a group, fit into a bigger picture of time or place. In history, this may lead into the stories of the past, often starting with one's own family or local area, and moving to the study of past cultures, to understand how other people were similar to, and different from, ourselves, and to realise how it was to live in a different era. Story and first-hand experience achieve this much more effectively than working only through the written word. Similar considerations apply for geography. For example, making and interpreting maps can help children see where they fit in terms of place. Comparing one's own neighbourhood with another highlights common needs and differences. Drawing on your children's own experience, visits and, where appropriate, family heritage brings history and geography alive and helps children explore and understand their own identity.

Art and music are associated especially with encouraging children's creativity. Both appreciation and composition engage modes of learning other than the linguistic and encourage responses at an emotional, often unconscious, level. As we saw in Chapter 7, language is not the natural language of feeling for young children. The kinaesthetic aspects of art and music help young children to express and explore feelings more easily, through creating new visual worlds or, in singing, being able to perform as part of a collective activity. Looking at a sculpture or hearing a piece of music can engage the learner at an experiential, less superficial level. Composing a picture in the style of an artist or a musical sequence with percussion encourages a child get 'inside' the creative process. More obviously, experiencing a wide range of art and music helps to extend children's cultural awareness and has the potential both to excite and to calm.

Gymnastics and dance provide the chance for exploration of the self, both physically and emotionally, again using a means of expression which young children enjoy. Inhibitions become more evident in Key Stage 2, especially when children become more self-conscious. So, many children who are keen on some types of movement, whether in team sport or a disco, become reluctant when exposed to the danger of ridicule or individual failure. However, PE enables many children to gain a positive sense of self-identity and learn social skills whether in co-operative or competitive games.

Design & Technology provides an obvious forum for children to be creative, though often there is insufficient time to take projects through to conclusion. Physical and space constraints tend to make this only an occasional activity rather than an approach to be adopted in other subject areas, such as designing a habitat for mini-beasts or making a medieval castle. While ICT has potential for SMSC, such as discovering about another culture through the internet or children taking much more control of their own learning, this remains largely unexploited in most schools. The introduction of entitlement to modern foreign languages in Key Stage 2 by 2010 has the potential of extending the level of children's cultural and linguistic awareness and of valuing the ability to speak more than one language.

Case study

Let the experience speak for itself

With twenty minutes to spare on a visit to Long Melford, in Suffolk, I took the children into the spectacular medieval church. Their response was complete silence, amazed at its grandeur and height. We could have listed all the features, or discussed the construction, but it seemed best to focus on experience and response. At times, information hinders the experience of mystery and wonder associated with SMSC.

RE syllabuses usually distinguish between:

- **awareness and response, knowledge and understanding and expression of personal beliefs; and**
- **explicit aspects, such as knowledge about beliefs and practices, and implicit ones, such as relationships, experiences and responses.**

The knowledge and the explicit aspects can contribute especially to moral and cultural development. For example, knowing how specific areas of a synagogue are used or the importance of holy books can help explain why faith is so central to many people's identity. However, RE contributes most to SMSC when linked to children's own practices and beliefs, so that they can identify common human needs rather than difference and what is alien. Learning by direct experience, by visiting places of worship, or meeting a member of a faith community, and through drama, art and music often helps to overcome initial embarrassment, maintains children's interest and embeds the learning. This contributes to all children's understanding and supports those for whom membership of a faith community is central to their identity. Be sensitive, and ask where you are not sure, but do not let uncertainty stop you from seeing RE as an important forum for enhancing your children's SMSC.

'Extended schools', with activities outside the main school day, may offer significant opportunities for SMSC. After-school and lunchtime clubs enable children to develop talents and interests, providing a chance for teachers and children to relate somewhat differently. Your school may also participate in local initiatives organised for gifted and talented children or those such as the Children's University, offering extension activities with children from other schools. Many of these contribute hugely to children's SMSC, but SMSC must not be relegated simply to optional, out-of-school sessions.

These two sections have considered the formal curriculum very briefly. However, once you look at the curriculum through the lens of SMSC, you will uncover many possible activities, most obviously as you plan your teaching.

Points for consideration and discussion

How can you plan to expect the unexpected?

To what extent will planning involve specific lessons or experiences?

How much does SMSC involve departing from your short-term plans?

How can one plan for what cannot be predicted?

Much of your course is likely to focus on planning and assessing short-term activities, often skill-related. One can rarely be sure what will prompt the types of experience or develop the qualities associated with SMSC. Planning for what may occur at any time seems tricky. It is useful to distinguish between provision planned in advance and situations where adults are prepared to exploit unexpected possibilities.

In this section, I discuss further the implications of the second and in the final section those for more formal planning to enhance SMSC.

An old army dictum states that 'No plan of action ever survives the first encounter with the enemy.' This is not to say that one can dispense with planning. Indeed, detailed planning is as essential in teaching as in the army – not that teaching is a battle, though it may sometimes feel like one! But teachers, like generals, must be flexible enough to respond to changed circumstances. It is unwise to plough on regardless, when you find you have misjudged the ability or the mood of a class – as we all have, many times. Ignoring a particular response from a child or a class may lose the opportunity for a moment of insight or self-awareness. You need to be prepared to alter any plan at short notice. As the following two stories illustrate, this may be at an inconvenient moment or without conscious planning.

Case studies

The Christmas play

I was due, as head, to introduce the Christmas play. The parents had gathered and I was helping with the last-minute adjustments to costumes and gathering the stragglers. One was Damien, a high-attaining Afro-Caribbean nine year old who found it difficult to control his temper. At the last minute, another child made a remark about Damien's colour and was told that this was inappropriate, before being taken to the hall. Only Damien and I were left and I knew that the whole school community was waiting. He asked why he had to put up with such remarks. Anxious to get him – and me – to the performance, I said that he shouldn't have to but that I thought he was likely to encounter such remarks quite often. So, he needed to work out when and how to challenge it, without making the situation worse for himself by being provoked into getting into trouble. I offered to talk further at another time, though we never did. From this intense conversation, we hurried into the hall, full of eager parents and their children dressed as animals and angels.

Freedom or happiness?

A dramatic moment came in a Year 6 class, where I was leading a discussion about the rights and wrongs of zoos. We had got beyond some simple opening statements and were starting to discuss whether caged animals were happy, when Brenda, a quiet but forceful girl, said, 'I think that zoos are wrong because freedom is always more important than comfort.' Neil was not due to speak but he could not contain himself. 'I don't agree with Brenda,' he said, 'you'd rather be secure with your mum even if you were enslaved.' The rest of the class, and I, listened, transfixed, as they debated, without coming to any conclusion, one of the oldest and most profound arguments in philosophy.

Points for consideration and discussion

Was my response appropriate in both these situations?

What were the preconditions which enabled the children to say what they did?

How, if at all, would you as the teacher have intervened differently?

While you cannot know whether, and when moments of significance will occur, you can create the environment, offer an opportunity or prompt a response which touches the child and provides the chance for deeper and more personal responses. However, schools can also mark particular events significant for an individual or group, such as birthdays, a new baby in the family and religious festivals. These help children to see that other people care about such events and markers of identity, which matter to them a great deal.

In Chapter 5, I suggested that creativity implies that the outcome is not known exactly in advance. A skilled practitioner, whether sculptor, gardener or teacher, starts with an idea of what she or he hopes to achieve but has the confidence to alter this, often only slightly, during the activity. So, a good teacher will plan particular activities, but try to foresee, and be prepared for, varied possibilities and be prepared to take advantage of an unexpected event or to follow a child's question or a comment. To do this successfully, especially in terms of SMSC, you must be willing to:

- **attend to your children's interests, experiences and responses;**
- **allow room for these to influence how lessons develop.**

This requires a constant assessment of children's state of learning and revising one's teaching accordingly. Remember that reciprocity – taking account of other people's responses – is one quality of a good learner: which all teachers should be.

It is tempting to think that SMSC is so elusive that you do not have to plan for it, especially if plans may have to change at short notice. However, unless teachers consciously plan for experiences and activities designed to enable children's SMSC, other pressures easily squeeze these out. So plan carefully, but be prepared to deviate from your plan.

What are the practical implications for medium-term planning?

You will be relieved to know that SMSC does not require another set of plans. Since your school will almost certainly have a planning format for medium- and short-term planning, I do not suggest specific formats. The detail of these is well covered in Chapter 2 of Jacques and Hyland (2003). This section suggests ways to include children's needs in relation to SMSC, whatever the format.

Planning should start with the sort of experience and outcomes you wish to achieve, finding activities to enable these, rather than the other way round. It is relatively easy to identify outcomes in terms of skills and knowledge, much harder in terms of values and attitudes. Yet there is a strong tradition of education working towards outcomes that cannot be quantified. The Plowden Report (DES, 1967, p187 paragraph 505) states that *a school is not merely a teaching shop, it must transmit values and attitudes,* and the Standards to Achieve QTS emphasise professional values and practice (SI) and knowledge and understanding (S2).

It is not for me to determine which outcomes are appropriate for you as they will depend to some extent on the values of the school, the community, the family and the individual. For instance, a Catholic school or Muslim parent may view children's faith and values as at least as important as reaching a particular level in tests. An appropriate aim for a group of children with behavioural difficulties may be to learn to control their anger, or for a talented pianist to improve her playing, while maintaining a breadth of interest.

However, your own beliefs and values will be one factor in your provision for SMSC being authentic. Teachers usually express these rather vaguely, if at all, such as 'wanting children to be happy' or 'their behaviour to improve'. The virtues and values outlined in Chapter 3 and the protective and transformational qualities in Chapter 6 make a good starting point in thinking about what you wish to achieve and what activities will lead to these. For example, virtues and values, such as co-operation, respect and understanding, may lead to activities involving responsible citizenship and global awareness. Valuing reflectiveness and insight may call for activities, discussion or silence to help children consider whether there is anything beyond the physical world; or creativity and playfulness for exploring an unfamiliar piece of software or construction materials.

Medium-term planning, usually outlining the content of your teaching over a period of several weeks, can take account of SMSC by highlighting specific experiences, which may have to be arranged well in advance, and by considering the possibilities in different subject areas and looking for cross-curricular opportunities.

Incorporating these in medium-term plans makes it easier to find space for them in short-term lesson plans.

The type of specific experiences likely to contribute to SMSC may include:

- **residential trips;**
- **visits to a museum, a place of worship or a historical site;**
- **inviting visitors with a particular expertise or experience, such as a parent, member of the local community, or an expert practitioner, such as a poet or an artist in residence.**

How you approach medium-term planning will vary between schools. If you are part of a team, maybe a Year or Key Stage group, depending on the size of the school, this has several advantages. It helps you, as a less experienced teacher, to draw on other colleagues' experience and wisdom. But you are likely to be more up-to-date in terms of curriculum requirements, so be prepared to contribute your own views. Working as a group helps to uncover possibilities, and possible drawbacks, which are not obvious when working on one's own — a case of collective learning being better than individual endeavour. SMSC (and other cross-curricular strands) are easily overlooked. Planning together, with individuals looking at medium-term planning from the perspective of cross-curricular themes, including SMSC, can help to avoid this.

What are the implications of short-term planning?

Identifying clear learning objectives or intentions in short-term planning helps to focus your mind on what you are hoping to achieve. Making these explicit to children is usually appropriate. However, this brings two risks:

- **if the learning objectives are only skills-based, both you and the children may concentrate too much on these, too little on processes and attitudes;**
- **if they are predetermined, this narrows the scope for creativity.**

It is easy to become bogged down by lesson plans which are too full of content. So, if your formal plans, especially short-term ones, are to enable, rather than hinder, teaching which enhances SMSC, leave some space for open-ended enquiry, reflection and discussion. Many schools have developed little symbols or shorthand to assist teachers in remembering particular approaches or needs in their short-term planning, such as VAK to remember to cater for different learning styles or PW for pair work. You may wish to use one to show where opportunities for SMSC may occur.

Do not forget to include opportunities for children to work in groups of different mixes and sizes.

Remember to plan for how other adults in the classroom can contribute to SMSC. Learning support staff often bring a range of expertise, such as creative abilities or awareness of the children's social and cultural background. Moreover, they can often form rather different relationships with children, which may make them sensitive to, or more able to respond to, children's difficulties. Yet often they are used only with one group, usually those who find learning difficult, or one activity. They can have a particular role in providing opportunities for discussion or creative activities, for looking in greater detail or for nurturing those who are vulnerable. As a resource for personal development, support staff are too often underused.

I hope that this has helped you to see the importance of planning being long term, cross-curricular and flexible. If thought of exclusively in small, lesson-sized units, it can overemphasise skills and underplay attitudes and values. If considered only in subject terms, it risks imposing artificial barriers and inhibiting the connectivity central to how children learn. If planning is overcrowded or inflexible, you risk missing moments of intense experience and greatest insight. Developing your children's positive values and attitudes is more important than covering every detail of what you are supposed to. But one essential factor in good provision for SMSC remains to be discussed: your own values, attitudes and qualities.

Recommended reading

Baldwin, P (2004) *With Drama in Mind*. Stafford: Network Educational Press. A very clear combination of the underlying research rationale and practical activities on why and how to teach through drama.

Claire, H (ed.) (2004) *Teaching Citizenship in Primary Schools*. Exeter: Learning Matters. A companion volume to this, with many useful case studies, reflecting how an area in some ways similar to SMSC fits into the curriculum.

Farnell, A and others (2003) *Opening Windows*. Nottingham: The Stapleford Centre. An interesting booklet on spiritual development, mainly but not exclusively from a Christian perspective, with Appendix 5 especially useful on activities.

Jacques, K and Hyland, R (eds) (2003) *Professional Studies: Primary Phase*. Exeter: Learning Matters. The chapter on Planning and Preparation for Teaching (pp7–32) offers a good outline of how to approach formal, especially short-term, planning.

Ofsted (2002) *The curriculum in successful primary schools*. www.ofsted.gov.uk/ publications HMI 553. A useful analysis of how good schools both concentrate on core subjects and encourage imagination and creativity, often through a thematic approach.

Wilson, A (ed.) (2005) *Creativity in Primary Education*. Exeter: Learning Matters. Chapters 3 to 14 suggest a wide range of activities in different subject areas to enhance creativity.

Other references

Claxton, G (2005) *An Intelligent Look at Emotional Intelligence*. London: Association of Teachers and Lecturers

DES (Department of Education and Science) (1967) *Children and their Primary Schools. (The Plowden Report)* London: HMSO

Gardner, H (1993) *Frames of Mind: the Theory of Multiple Intelligences*. London: Fontana

10 LINKING SPIRITUAL, MORAL, SOCIAL AND CULTURAL DEVELOPMENT WITH YOUR OWN PROFESSIONAL DEVELOPMENT

By the end of this chapter you should:

- *recognise the importance of your own values and beliefs and have reflected further on why these matter so much;*
- *have considered the challenges in making good provision for SMSC and how to meet these;*
- *thought about why it is so important to look after yourself and how to do so;*
- *have considered ways of enabling continuing professional development which enhance your children's SMSC and your own enjoyment of teaching.*

This will help you to meet Standards:
- → *S 1.1, 1.2, 1.3, 1.5, 1.7*

Like many other teachers, I share Ofsted's (2004, p4) view that *most teachers would see [pupils' SMSC development] as the heart of what education is all about – helping pupils grow and develop as people.* You will not agree with everything that I have written. That's fine, but I hope to have:

- convinced you that education involves something far more profound, elusive and life-changing than academic results;
- offered you new insights into spiritual, moral, social and cultural development;
- reassured you that much of what you do already helps to enhance your children's **SMSC**.

However, you may think, 'This talk about SMSC is all very well, but how can I manage this when I have all my planning to fit in, resources to prepare, my own family to look after and I'm shattered every evening?' In this chapter, I try to:

- summarise why you are so important as a teacher;
- explore how you can deal with the conflicting pressures;
- consider the qualities you need to enhance **SMSC**; and
- suggest the implications for continuing professional development (**CPD**).

Points for consideration and discussion

What are the key messages about spiritual, moral, social and cultural development?

What are the implications for you as a teacher?

What roles for a teacher can you identify other than deliverer of information?

Why are you as a teacher so important?

As a teacher, you are important. Part of the excitement of teaching is to create a world of opportunities, with the power to transform and create. Whatever government policy, the National Curriculum, your headteacher or this book say, these only support, or hinder, what happens at the most important point – the interaction between learner and teacher. Good provision for SMSC provides a structure within which children can:

- **explore, and seek answers, to the most important questions in life: Who am I? Where do I fit in? and Why we are here?**
- **develop values and qualities that form the basis of their character and how they act;**
- **learn to regulate their emotional responses so that they relate to other people appropriately;**
- **have respect for their own, and other, cultures, beliefs and values.**

These depend more on the quality, and qualities, of teachers and the relationships they form with children than immaculate plans, wonderful buildings or the latest technology.

The child's constantly changing sense of self, identity or narrative is both affected by, and helps to create, his or her understanding of the world. Relationships, in every aspect of school life and beyond, are crucial to how this is created and sustained in an often unconscious process more subtle than the transfer of information and acquisition of skills. The teacher's role is to be a facilitator, a supporter, a nurturer and a guide at least as much as a deliverer.

Coles (1989, p119) writes, *the ultimate test of a person's worth as a doctor or teacher or lawyer has to do not only with what he or she knows, but with how he or she behaves with another person, the patient or student or client.* Just as children have to 'walk the talk', teachers must not simply talk a good game. The power of example and unconscious learning means that who, and how, you are as a teacher, how you respond to different types of experiences and how you regulate your emotional responses, matters more than acquiring a toolkit of skills and techniques or the content of what you deliver. Even very young children are extremely astute in recognising a mismatch between what adults say and what they do. If you are sympathetic to those in trouble, children will pick that up without you necessarily telling them. If you show respect for different cultural traditions, children are more likely to do the same. If you demonstrate curiosity, creativity or imagination, this prompts children to follow suit.

Points for consideration and discussion

What are the challenges within the formal curriculum in enhancing SMSC?

What are the personal and emotional challenges?

Who can help and support you in meeting these challenges?

We saw that many children find moral and social development difficult because of mixed, confusing messages. You may feel similarly confused, especially with:

- **a system and a curriculum with a great deal of content to be covered and a strong emphasis on measurable outcomes;**
- **a feeling of inadequacy stemming from concern about the children's behaviour and your responses, and a workload that may leave you worn out or feeling that on top of everything else SMSC is just too much and too complicated.**

Working within these constraints will be easier if you can find opportunities within the curriculum for breadth, balance and space, and in your own professional life for nurture as well as challenge.

No one going into teaching in primary schools should doubt that it is very demanding. It is hard to keep personal development at the front of your mind when struggling to keep a class of stroppy Year 6s on task or desperately trying to cover everything you are supposed to. We saw in Chapter 3 how children's behaviour affects your emotional responses. This commonly leads to feelings of inadequacy. Understanding how fundamental for all learning it is for children (and adults) to feel safe, in an environment with consistent relationships and high but achievable expectations is the first step towards working out what to do. Recognising why some children respond and behave as they do will help you not always to blame either yourself or the children when things are not going well. Aggressive or withdrawn behaviour is often a symptom of difficulties which may affect your own responses and only some of which you can influence.

The learning environment you create can help to provide both nurture and challenge, but it is always a combination of what both children and teachers bring to it. So, when things are tough, it is often worth looking at, and adapting, the curriculum. If it is too dull, introduce more variety; if too demanding, more nurturing and if too full, a little space.

Remember that much of what you do in the normal run of teaching enhances SMSC without constant, conscious planning. This includes the relationships formed, the care for a child's distress, the sharing of a life-enhancing experience and hundreds of other small actions. While we can never hope to get SMSC absolutely 'right', teachers are for many children one of the most secure and supportive points in a confusing world. Never forget that, even when feeling low or inadequate, you are for many children a beacon of security and hope.

> *What are people looking for when you stand before them as a teacher? Not for what you say. Half the time they do not understand you anyway. They are looking for you. You are the message ... Like it or not, we — mean, selfish, and unfaithful — are signs of faith for them, signs confirming also that we are human. And it is at times like that, perhaps, that we need others, maybe our own colleagues, as support when our own human weakness comes through.* (Hall, 1986, p7)

What support is available in an environment with often conflicting and confusing pressures?

The challenges of making good provision for SMSC make collaboration and dialogue with colleagues, one of Pollard and Tann's (1994, pp9–10) features of a reflective teacher, especially important. We have seen that learning is a social as well as an individual activity and the importance of interdependence. Teaching can be surprisingly isolated, given that you are surrounded by people. The camaraderie and mutual support is one notable feature of good primary schools. While developing your pedagogy is inevitably to some extent an individual journey, draw on the wisdom and support available in your school and outside, especially from those whom you trust, most of whom will offer this willingly. If you are having a hard time, don't keep it to yourself – when you are unsure about what to do, go and talk about it with someone you trust, and if one small thing might help, then ask for it.

We have seen how your expectations of children influence their aspirations and what they can achieve. Similarly, your own sense of self, as a teacher, is influenced by, and influences, the expectations of others and of yourself. Your own identity as a teacher can easily be self-fulfilling and affect how you teach, just as treating children as passive or inadequate learners is likely to make them so. To think of teaching as a conveyor belt, with parts to be assembled, may make you teach like that. If you see your role more like a sculptor, actively transforming children's lives, you may make more mistakes but your influence will ultimately be greater. If such identity is negative, it impacts adversely both on your own motivation and on children's learning. If it is positive, and you believe in what you do, this benefits both your children and yourself, making it more likely that you will enhance children's understanding of themselves.

Just as a good learning environment provides a mood and climate supportive to the child, enhancing children's SMSC is much easier where the school culture and ethos is in tune with your own values and beliefs. Positive feedback from colleagues, from parents and from children can help you to develop the coherent personal narrative as a teacher which will help your children to do so as learners. To work with colleagues who share your interests, or at least are not unsympathetic, makes planning and teaching in ways that enhance SMSC much easier. When on school experience, you may feel uncomfortable with some aspects of what happens in class or the whole school. All you can do, realistically, is to accept and learn from these. However, when looking for jobs, consider, if you can, whether the school:

- **makes explicit that it takes the personal development of children and adults seriously in practice;**
- **has at least some teachers whom you feel you can work with, and learn from.**

Where you are out of sympathy with your school's ethos and values, you may do better to look elsewhere.

Points for consideration and discussion

How would you describe the approach to SMSC of one school you have visited on school experience?

Which are the most important factors influencing this?

If you were appointed to teach there, what aspects of this approach would you welcome? Which would you hope to influence?

Your headteacher is one person to whom you can look for support, especially where children's personal development is a priority. If you are lucky, s/he will welcome new ideas and encourage innovative approaches. However, headteachers are busy people and other senior staff have their own priorities. The mentor appointed to support you when you are newly qualified may be able to offer valuable support. However, those most likely to do so are those with an interest in SMSC themselves, which is more a question of personality and interest than of role. So, search out soul-mates among your colleagues, especially those with whom you co-operate at the planning stage.

Unless you are unlucky, your school will provide a nurturing environment. But you must find ways to nurture yourself, not only for your own sake, but because it will help you to maintain your motivation as a teacher and make you a better one. Looking after yourself matters not only for you and for your family; in doing so you are making it more likely that your children's SMSC will be enhanced. A teacher who is crotchety, or disillusioned, or worn out may still be able to teach subtraction or spelling adequately, but this affects provision for SMSC much more.

You have a responsibility to look after yourself both physically and emotionally by:

- **recognising you can't do everything, so try to prioritise what is most important;**
- **finding space to do what nurtures you, whether it is painting or cycling, visiting friends or knitting, watching the TV or clubbing;**
- **enjoying a life outside teaching with your friends and your family.**

While they may be interested in what you do, teachers (like other groups) tend to get obsessive about their work, so remember not to go on about teaching too much.

Children need structure if they are to flourish. You are no different, except that it is up to you to maintain a structure to nurture yourself. How you do this will depend on other commitments, but it can help to establish rules, such as ensuring that you:

- **leave school by a set time each evening;**
- **make sure that you eat and drink properly;**
- **spend at least one evening a week doing something you really enjoy;**
- **keep at least one day per weekend clear for activities unassociated with teaching.**

Of course, such rules may need to be broken occasionally, but try to make that the exception.

Points for consideration and discussion

What were the qualities of teachers who have influenced you most?

Which qualities in a teacher are especially important in enhancing children's SMSC?

What sort of teacher do you hope to be in two, or five, or twenty years' time?

Which qualities in a teacher are especially important?

Teachers who enhance children's personal development show many of the qualities, both protective and transformational, from which children benefit. You will have to be emotionally resilient to protect yourself against pressure and criticism. For example, if you adopt my suggestions about finding space for children to reflect or about grouping, you may have to defend yourself quite robustly. And you will meet many children and parents with value systems that conflict with your own and the school's. Resourcefulness and reflectiveness will help create opportunities for SMSC, for instance by looking out for resources which widen the children's social and cultural awareness through literacy, or thinking about how to extend their spiritual and moral experience through practical engagement in real-life situations which may challenge their assumptions.

The most intriguing of the 4Rs in this context is reciprocity. One remarkable aspect of spiritual development is that it challenges the idea that teaching is a one-way process. Education is often thought of as resulting only in children being changed. However, relationships influence, and change, both partners, so that you are, as a teacher, constantly changing. Or at least you should be! As adults, we have much to learn from children, such as the ability to live in the present, to appreciate the simple things of life, to be uninhibited in our questions. So, one essential quality in making good provision for SMSC is the humility to recognise what we have to learn both from other teachers and from children.

Provision that enhances SMSC requires creativity and flexibility. Be brave enough to take risks, by rearranging the furniture, having music playing in class or teaching your children to meditate or engage in philosophical discussion. If you are to be creative, you must be prepared to take some chances, in a risk-averse culture. Being playful may entail you moving away from the script, and being critical of current orthodoxies may not make you popular. If you retain your curiosity, you will have to learn to live with ambiguity, uncertainty and paradox. Just as a child will be wary of exercising these qualities except in the right environment, you should be careful, but brave enough to do so when you can. This is easy for me to say, but much harder to do, so check before you do anything too extravagant or risky.

Enhancing children's SMSC is helped by remembering, and re-living, how hard it is to learn something new.

Case study

Learning to sing as an adult

As a little boy, I was never taught to pitch a note properly. When I was about 10, I was instructed to mouth the words and make no noise. Understandably, I learnt that I was a non-singer. At the age of 40, I decided to try and remedy this. A wonderful teacher ran classes for men like me, trying to get us to lose some of our deeply entrenched inhibitions, by combining singing with actions, by having a go without the fear of ridicule. I graduated to a non-singers' choir and gained considerable pleasure from singing in a group. Having told the teachers and children how hard I had found this learning, it was appropriate at an assembly when I was leaving the school that the music teacher encouraged me to 'lead' everyone in the chorus of a favourite song.

The newspaper columns that describe 'My Favourite Teacher' usually cite an infectious passion for learning and attention to the individual child. Unless you remain interested and passionate about learning, you will not fire your children's enthusiasm and will not develop as fully as a teacher as you might. So, I encourage you to share your own enthusiasms – for the clarinet or Chelsea, for gardening or the Greek islands – with children and colleagues. In particular, be prepared to share your experience as a parent or a painter, in a factory or a farm. This is both interesting and helps children to see how adults have shaped their own lives and identities.

Teaching is something you can never 'get absolutely right' – so even experienced teachers are always looking for ways to improve. In the final section, we consider the implications of SMSC for your professional development and how you can sustain and develop both the qualities and the identity that makes you both a better and a better motivated teacher.

How can you develop your pedagogy in relation to SMSC?

Gaining QTS is only one step on the journey towards becoming a good teacher. It involves a journey of self-discovery, a personal odyssey where your own professional development is never complete. In a sense, this whole book has been about continuing professional development (CPD) because good provision for SMSC involves constant reflection on your values and adjustments to your pedagogy.

CPD is often seen as consisting primarily of staff meetings, INSET days and courses, usually focusing on skills, techniques and activities. While necessary and useful, these are not enough, for three main reasons:

- such courses as there are about **SMSC** tend to focus on a particular activity or idea, such as circle time or emotional literacy;
- few make much use of enactive and iconic learning;
- they rarely help you to reflect on your own practice and pedagogy in the classroom.

Much of your course input will relate to the skills and techniques which help in planning lessons and classroom management, with a particular emphasis on literacy and numeracy. As a student, and soon after you are qualified, you are likely, sensibly, to concentrate mainly on the core subjects and planning for, and creating, an orderly and purposeful classroom environment. In particular, you will probably focus strongly on what you, as a teacher, do and the activities you set up. However, try to have the confidence to make links between subjects or the flexibility to respond to unexpected opportunities. Unless you keep in mind the broader issues discussed in this book, you may create an identity, or narrative, for yourself as a teacher which loses sight of what is most important in children's learning and, maybe, to you.

Do go on such courses related to SMSC as are available, though your induction programme and courses provided by your local authority will probably not give this a high priority. When you find appropriate courses, your school may be reluctant to release you if your class has to be covered, especially if these are not part of the formal induction programme. SMSC rarely appears as a major part of a School Improvement Plan. While you may find it easier to be released for short, practical courses, such as those related to emotional literacy, the really deep-seated learning which will change your practice takes place when courses reach beyond the cognitive level.

Case study

A never-to-be-forgotten afternoon

Almost 20 years ago, I was on a 20-day course on cultural diversity. We gathered for the last afternoon ready to wind down, fairly sure how to improve what happened back in school. The last speaker launched into us, saying how, as white teachers, we had no idea how much racism black and minority ethnic teachers had to endure. Whenever anyone suggested what they might do, he found a way of saying that this was just a way of maintaining the status quo. We later heard that this was unplanned. We all left shattered. This was not an experience I would recommend, but no other course has ever affected me so much, because it touched me at an emotional level.

We have seen that young children learn through enactive and iconic modes, as well as through language. For you to develop as a teacher requires more than gathering information and skills, but understanding at a deeper level. Dewey (cited in Schon, p 7) writes that a student teacher *[has] to 'see' on his own behalf and in his own way the relations between means and ends employed and results achieved. Nobody else can see for him, and he can't see just by being 'told', although the right kind of telling may guide his seeing and thus help him see what he needs to see.* There is a particular irony for me as an author that language is inadequate to reach the deeper levels of improving as a teacher. The general principles you can learn from a course or a book like this are more useful in helping you to recognise good practice than in actually teaching better. So I have used stories, examples and questions to try and encourage enactive and iconic learning, but the most valuable professional development will be that in your own school and classroom.

Watching other teachers at work is one of the best ways of improving your pedagogy. While opportunities are relatively rare, using non-contact time, whether as an NQT or in planning, preparation and assessment time, makes this possible. When you have the chance to observe more experienced teachers, you may be encouraged to look at lesson delivery, but you will learn more by looking at the process, rather than the content, asking questions like these:

- **How did the teacher create an environment which encouraged children to develop particular qualities?**
- **What did she do to encourage that group to be more thoughtful or that quiet child to speak up?**
- **How would I have responded to that child's off-beat, but interesting, comment?**

These small, but important, aspects of pedagogy are those which help to enhance SMSC. Learning what is difficult is usually more effective with someone else and where neither person feels under pressure to put on a performance. Peer mentoring – where you and a colleague watch each other teaching and each gives feedback – may be possible. If you are brave enough, ask someone to video you. This is rather unnerving but it teaches you a great deal about how you teach and how to improve your teaching.

Pollard and Tann (1994, pp9–10) highlight engagement in classroom enquiry as one feature of a reflective teacher. You may think of this as being about engaging in research, which at some point you may wish to do. However, Schon (1987) distinguishes between reflection **on** action and reflection **in** action. The former is like a separate activity, before and after one acts, to plan and evaluate what one is doing. Reflection in action is more like a way of being aware of and seeing yourself as you teach and is the best form of classroom enquiry, getting feedback about how children respond to your teaching. In terms of SMSC, children will provide endless feedback, if you attend to their interests and their struggles and watch their responses. Watch what happens in the classroom and around the school. This may seem impossible within a busy classroom, but you will improve with practice. When taking the register, notice children's responses. Step back occasionally in the classroom and watch an individual or a group. Note down moments where a child shows particular insight, worry or joy. And look out for how children respond in assembly, on the playground and as they arrive at, and leave, school. All these will give you clues about how the curriculum, formal, informal and hidden is influencing them. And the resulting understanding is one of the most valuable ways of learning to improve your provision for SMSC.

Points for consideration and discussion

How else can you manage to attend to children's responses?

How can you use enactive learning to develop as a teacher?

What three main messages will you take away from reading this book?

However, to embed new practices, you must try them for yourself – enactive learning. As Black et al. (2002, p21) indicate, *the effective development of formative assessment ... only come(s) about if each teacher finds his or her own ways of incorporating the lessons and ideas ... into her or his own patterns of classroom work.* The professional development likely to make the greatest long-term impact will involve you in:

- **reflecting on your own practice;**
- **challenging your own assumptions;**
- **working out what went well and what did not;**
- **trying out new approaches;**
- **evaluating their success.**

These processes of monitoring, evaluating and revising practice based on self-reflection and other people's experience are among Pollard and Tann's features of reflective teaching. Relating these to your own context and practice is what will help you most to develop your own pedagogy and identity as teacher and constantly improve the provision which enhances your children's SMSC and your fulfillment as a teacher. However, this is not easy, especially on your own, with other, often conflicting, priorities. Try to find others to support you when you can and do not expect instant results. Appropriate outcomes in terms of SMSC, as learner or teacher, take a long time to come to fruition, but they are more satisfying when they do.

We have almost reached the end of this part of the journey. I hope that you relish the prospect of seeing your children mature and flourish, not only as readers or artists, but in their confidence or their ability to relate to new people. Recognising your own part in the growth of children's sense of self and identity is one of the wonderful privileges of teaching.

You will, of course, draw from this book your own messages, but I end with three which are relevant to children's learning. First, in the words of Plutarch, a poet of Ancient Rome, *the mind is not a vessel to be filled but a fire to be lighted.* Second, as Donaldson (1992, p20) writes, *Some kinds of knowledge are in the light of full awareness. Others are in the shadows, on the edge of the bright circle. Still others are in the darkness beyond.* Finally, in the words of Tokutomi Roka, (quoted in Carr, 1984, before p1):

It is the death of the spirit we must fear.
To believe only what one is taught and brought up to believe,
to repeat what one has been told to say,
to do only what one is expected to do,
to live like a factory-made doll,
to lose confidence in one's independence
and the hope of better things –

that is the death of the spirit.

Recommended reading

Donaldson, M (1992) *Human Minds: an exploration*. London: Penguin. A clear account by a psychologist of the complexity of how young children learn with many echoes of the ideas in this book. Chapters 1 and 2 are especially good.

Pollard, A and Tann, S (1994) *Reflective Teaching in the Primary School*. London: Cassell. Interesting ideas on the link between teachers' identity and how children learn, with practical activities designed to help you explore this (especially Chapter 4, pp57–84).

Other references

Carr, JL (1984) *The Harpole Report*. London: Penguin

Coles, R (1989) *The call of stories*. Boston, MA: Houghton Mifflin

Donaldson, M (1984) *Children's Minds*. London: Flamingo

Hall, M (1986) *Education through encounter – a bridge quite near* (The Hockerill Lecure, 1986). Frinton-on-Sea: Hockerill Educational Foundation (available via hockerill.trust@ntlworld.com)

Ofsted (2004) *Promoting and evaluating pupils' spiritual, moral, social and cultural development*. www.ofsted.gov.uk/publications HMI 2125

Schon, D (1987) *Educating the Reflective Practitioner*. San Fransisco, CA: Jossey Bass

SOME CHILDREN'S BOOKS ESPECIALLY USEFUL FOR SMSC

There is a huge range of books, both fiction and non-fiction, which deal well with the questions raised by SMSC. This list contains some you may find useful.

Almond, D (1998) *Skellig*. London: Hodder

Almond, D (2000) *Heaven Eyes*. London: Hodder

Almond, D (2003) *The Fire Eaters*. London: Hodder

Browne, A (1992) *Gorilla*. London: Walker Books

Browne, A (1996) *Willy the Champ*. London: Walker Books

Browne, A (1999) *Voices in the Park*. London: Picture Corgi

Browne, A (2004) *Into the Forest*. London: Walker Books

Browne, E (1994) *Handa's Surprise*. London: Walker Books

Child, L (2000) *Clarice Bean, That's Me!* London: Orchard Books

Child, L (2004) *I Am Too Absolutely Small for School*. London: Orchard Books

Cooper, H (1998) *Pumpkin Soup*. London: Random House

Hoffman, M and Binch, C (1991) *Amazing Grace*. London: Frances Lincoln

Impey, R and Bell Corfield, R (1997) *Feather Pillows*. London: Collins

Innocenti, R and McEwan, I (2004) *Rose Blanche*. London: Red Fox

Isherwood, S (1994) *My Grandad*. Oxford: Oxford University Press

Lewis, K (1995) *My Friend Harry*. London: Walker Books

McKee, D (1990) *Not Now, Bernard*. London, Red Fox

Morpurgo, M (1996) *The Butterfly Lion*. London: Harper Collins

Morpurgo, M (1999) *Kensuke's Kingdom*. London: Egmont

Nicholls, J and Cockcroft, J (2002) *Billywise*. London: Bloomsbury

Poole, J and Barrett, A (2005) *Anne Frank*. London: Hutchinson

Sendak, M (1993) *Where the Wild Things Are*. London: Bodley Head

Serrailler, I (1982) *The Silver Sword*. London: Puffin Books

Varley, S (1992) *Badger's Gift*. London: Picture Lions

Waddell, M and Benson, P (1992) *Owl Babies*. London: Walker Books

How do I feel about . . . (series) *Loneliness and Making Friends, Bullies and Gangs, Looking after Myself, Dealing with Racism, When People Die, Our New Baby, My Stepfamily, My Parents' Divorce, Being Jealous, Being Angry*. London: Watts